CW01658572

St. Clare of Assisi

Light from the Cloister

ST. CLARE OF ASSISI

LIGHT FROM THE CLOISTER

BRET THOMAN, OFS

WITH A FOREWORD BY
ROSELLA CHIARA MANCINELLI, OSC

AND AN AFTERWORD BY
MURRAY BODO, OFM

TAN Books
Charlotte, North Carolina

St. Clare of Assisi: Light From the Cloister copyright © 2017 Bret Thoman

All rights reserved. With the exception of short excerpts used in articles and critical reviews, no part of this work may be reproduced, transmitted, or stored in any form whatsoever, printed or electronic, without the prior written permission of the publisher.

Unless otherwise noted, Scripture quotations are from the Revised Standard Version—Second Catholic Edition (Ignatius Edition), copyright © 2006 National Council of the Churches of Christ in the United States of America. Used by permission. All rights reserved.

Excerpts from *The Lady: Clare of Assisi: Early Documents* translated and edited by Regis J. Armstrong, O.F.M. Cap. reprinted by permission of New City Press, Hyde Park, NY. www.newcitypress.com

Cover design by David Ferris Design

Cover image: St. Clare Embraces the Body of St. Francis at the Convent of San Damiano, 1297-99 (fresco), Giotto di Bondone (c.1266-1337) / San Francesco, Upper Church, Assisi, Italy / Bridgeman Images

Library of Congress Control Number: 2017937644

ISBN: 978-1-5051-0971-9

Published in the United States by
TAN Books
P.O. Box 410487
Charlotte, NC 28241
www.TANBooks.com

Printed and bound in the United States of America

This book is dedicated to my daughter, Claremarie. It was also written for her.

It is my hope, desire, and prayer that you discover your own "light." And when God reveals it to you, be faithful to it, never let go of it, struggle to keep it, and safeguard it as that most precious Pearl.

May the intercession, spirit, and example of your namesake, St. Clare, guide you, inspire you, move you, and make you enthusiastic in all you do in your own life's journey.

Hear, my [daughter], your father's instruction,
and reject not your mother's teaching (see Prv 1:8).

The light shines in the darkness,
and the darkness has not overcome it.
JOHN 1:5

CONTENTS

FOREWORD

Mother Rosella Chiara, OSC

TO enter into a book is always an experience of "encounter": with a story, with faces, with the author, and even with oneself. The book which you, dear brother or sister reader, are about to begin is, on the surface, an encounter with the person and charism of Santa Chiara of Assisi. But it is an encounter with not only her but others as well, for the book you are about to read weaves together various stories and faces.

You will, first of all, encounter Chiara: the woman of Assisi who was called to be "light from the cloister." You will walk with her as she courageously renounces a life of worldly privileges—knights and chivalry, land and wealth, status and nobility—and chooses, instead, to become the first woman follower of Francis with just one privilege: that of poverty.

Next, you will encounter the community of sisters in San Damiano. You will meet other women who, like Chiara, made the decision to leave their families and embrace life in community and the hardships of poverty. In this, Chiara and the women of San Damiano chose the joy of walking in the footsteps of the poor and humble Christ.

However, if you go deeper, you may discover that the faces of these characters from eight centuries ago are not very different from those who continue to embrace this form of Clarian life: like us—today's Clarisse (Poor Clares) who still strive to receive and live the legacy of Chiara of Assisi.

Our community is comprised of twenty sisters of varying ages (from thirty to ninety-four!) who live in a small village in the central Italian region of the Marches. Our origins, in simplicity and joy, testify to a contemplative and evangelical life lived through following in the footsteps of Francis and Chiara.

Our days are punctuated by liturgical prayer, immersion in silence, moments of recreation, and listening to the Word. Underlying everything is intense fraternal sharing and humble daily work (we make Eucharistic hosts for churches and stitch habits for the Friars Minor). Ours is a simple presence, though rich in relationship with the Lord and with friendships with the friars as well as our brothers and sisters in our local community and beyond.

We live vows of simplicity, though today we have been called to an even more radical poverty due to the 2016 earthquakes that damaged several parts of our monastery. As a result, we have been forced to accept new living quarters in the guesthouse, where our space (so important to our way of life) has been greatly reduced.

Returning to the book at hand, there are other faces as well: those of other characters and personages from Chiara's time and place come to life on these pages—her mother and father, uncles and sisters, neighbors and relatives, knights and nuns, Francis and the brothers, strong-willed abbesses, bishops, and popes.

Further, if you read between the lines, you might also be able to discern (especially if you know him as we do) the face of Bret and his family in certain characters. But in this book, there are many faces of people like him: those who have discovered a reality that fascinates and amazes, not only because of the testimony of a choice of total surrender to God, but also due to the fraternal welcome that engages and becomes sharing, and which, in turn, calls one to a more authentic and profound faith.

But there is One who unites all these faces: that of Christ himself. It was this face of Christ, on the crucifix at San Damiano, that inspired Francis to leave his bourgeois family behind and follow him in simplicity and poverty; it was this face of Christ that inspired Chiara to leave her own noble family and do the same; and it is this face that has inspired so many—all those, throughout the centuries, who have followed the challenge of the Gospel: "If you would be perfect, go, sell what you possess and give to the poor, and you will have treasure in heaven; and come, follow me" (Mt 19:21).

In the end, this book intricately weaves together all these faces and stories. Indeed, what stands out is the underlying theme of relationships as Bret Thoman explores how Chiara related to her earthly mother and father, to Francis, to her sisters, but especially to the Father. For the spiritual life flourishes when it is engaged with others: in a religious fraternity like ours or that of the friars; in a holy family, the domestic church, like that of Bret, his wife, and children; in a lay order like the Secular Franciscan Order; or in so many other ecclesial communities now proliferating throughout the Catholic Church.

Finally, within the lines of this book, it is our hope and prayer that you, dear reader, will be able to see your own face. May this book be like a mirror for you, and may the light of the Gospel—lived and reflected so brightly by Chiara—illuminate you and reflect your own story and calling.

And as you begin your journey in the life of Chiara, know that we—the Poor Clare Sisters who have been called to safeguard her legacy and story—will be accompanying you in prayer as you walk with St. Clare of Assisi: Light From the Cloister.

Mother Rosella Chiara, OSC

AUTHOR'S NOTE

HOW do we know anything about this woman who was born over eight centuries ago, in the High Middle Ages, when written records were transcribed by hand, were sometimes unreliable, and often did not survive the ravages of history? Most modern historians base their knowledge of St. Clare primarily on two main sources.

The first is known as the *Legend of St. Clare.* Written soon after the saint's death, its author is unknown, although most scholars believe it was Thomas of Celano, a Franciscan friar who had previously written two *Vitae* (Lives) of St. Francis.

However, medieval Vitae are often unreliable, as they are hagiography—uncritical and overly reverent legends that regularly employed hyperbole, embellishments, and exaggerations to increase devotion and strengthen the cult of the particular saint. In this case, however, history would end up vindicating Thomas's *Legend of St. Clare.*

Shortly after Clare's funeral, Pope Innocent IV sent a letter to the archbishop of Spoleto, Bartolomeo, to begin hearing testimonies to ascertain the holiness of Clare's life. On November 24, 1253, the first hearings were held in San Damiano where witnesses (fifteen sisters who lived with Clare in the monastery, a woman who was a childhood friend of Clare, and four men from Assisi who had known her when she was a child), under sworn oath, responded to questions framed around three main themes:

Clare's childhood and her embrace of religious life; her sanctity within San Damiano; and miracles ascribed to her intercession.

Fortunately, the transcripts—referred to as the "Process of Canonization"—were discovered in the early twentieth century in a library in Florence, having found their way from a Poor Clare monastery in Tuscany. Remarkably, the sworn testimonies of the "Process "confirmed, by and large, what was in the *Legend.* Indeed, many of the accounts of the witnesses are so similar to what is in the *Legend,* it is believed that the author had surely interviewed them as well. Thus, the *Legend* is more than a legend and is considered a reliable source for knowing about the life of St. Clare.

In addition to these two main sources, there are a handful of extant writings by Clare, including her Rule, her Testament, a blessing, and several letters. Moreover, there are some other secondary sources that also refer to St. Clare (such as Thomas of Celano's first biography of St. Francis). Together, these sources offer us invaluable information and give us a general overview of her life.

In earlier Franciscan studies, Clare often appeared in the background of biographies about St. Francis as merely a chapter or, worse, a footnote. It is true that Clare described herself as a follower of Francis, as the *pianticella* (little plant) of Francis. Yet, she deserves better.

Today, thankfully, this has changed. With the ancient sources in hand, modern writers and biographers have been able to reconstruct the life of St. Clare. In the early 1990s, to mark the eighth centenary of her birth, there were a number of studies on her life, and Clare received the warranted attention she merits: as foundress of a unique order within the Franciscan family and the Catholic Church, as the first woman to write a Rule approved by the Church, as a stalwart defender of poverty, as a woman who had received a unique calling, and as someone who was misunderstood by many and yet remained orthodox. Yet the details—both in the medieval sources as well as in the modern studies—remain vague.

What follows is not a work of academia, objective biography, or straight history (there are plenty of good studies on St. Clare already out there: see "For Further Reading" at end of the book). Instead, I have sought something else: an historical narrative.

I have (perhaps boldly) set out to explore what was at the heart of this still little known medieval saint. I sought to delve into her desires and inspirations, her emotions and her loves, and in that way, to discover what fired her indomitable desire and lifelong quest for Gospel poverty. Thus, this is a portrait of a woman that is highly subjective and deeply personal.

In taking such an approach, it was necessary to fill in the blanks, and in so doing, I added a considerable amount of conjecture. Thus, this book should not be taken literally in its entirety, as it is a blend of biography and historical fiction, of facts and speculation. In some ways, the disclaimer that precedes some movies or television programs is warranted here: the following is based on a true story.

Hence, in order to distinguish what is based on historical facts from my own speculation, just as I did in my first book, *St. Francis of Assisi: Passion, Poverty, and the Man Who Transformed the Catholic Church*, I employed notes.

Whenever a detail in the book is known to be an historical fact, there is a note to cite the source; if there is no note, the reader can assume that it is from my imagination. Further, given that most of what we know about St. Clare comes from the *Legend*, I included the said text at the end of each chapter dealing with that episode of Clare's life.

Finally, before you begin your journey into the story of St. Clare, I recall the words of Sister Benvenuta, a follower of Clare who lived with her in San Damiano and testified during her canonization process: "No one could even talk about how holy [Clare] became unless the Holy Spirit helped them to speak." It is my hope that the words of this book were, likewise, divinely inspired. But it is my greater prayer that you, the reader, will ask the Holy Spirit, as well as the intercession of St. Clare, to guide you as you now enter into her life.

Bret Thoman, OFS

PREFACE

THE first time I ever entered a Poor Clare church was in 2004. I was with my wife, Katia, in the postcard-perfect medieval hill town of San Severino at the base of the Apennine Mountains in central Italy. We were with a group of Italians on a pilgrimage to the Franciscan places within the bucolic region of the Marches led by the provincial minister, Fr. Ferdinando Campana, OFM.

We were there to meet the sisters who would tell us the tale of how St. Francis visited their town long before in 1219. His ship had just landed in the port city of Ancona after his famed visit to the Holy Land when he encountered the Muslim Sultan, and he was returning to Assisi. He was carrying on his shoulders a sheep that he would leave in the custody of a community of holy sisters.[1] Those nuns eventually took the Rule of St. Clare, and the present community traced their lineage directly to them.

As I sat in the church waiting for Evening Prayer to begin, I recall looking beyond the grate into the sacred enclosure behind the altar and tabernacle. As it was a cloistered monastery, there was a sense of mystery; yet, it seemed, nevertheless, somehow inviting and welcoming.

Bells rang and soon there was movement. Sporadically at first, then in greater numbers, nuns in full habit and headdress began quietly filling the choral space. They were all ages, and some of the young ones tenderly accompanied the older ones with canes to their respective places.

Though it was difficult to see clearly through the grate, I could sense that they were joyful and they seemed special. It was as if an entire world was back there, enclosed and self-contained.

Moments later, an organ began playing and the chanting started. Wow. Their melodic voices were warm, gentle, and consoling. Their song was like perfume that permeated the space and exuded vitality and freshness. When Vespers was over, the nuns knelt and quietly said a prayer. Then, through the same door that they had entered, they retreated just as solemnly as they had arrived. I sat there for a moment struck by what I had just experienced. I felt as if I had been transported to a place somewhere else, where all was pure, lovely, and gracious.

Our small group was then summoned to a large room in the guesthouse next to the church where we were served a scrumptious and filling dinner prepared by the nuns. After the homemade tiramisu, I imagined it was time to go. Instead, a large door opened up and the nuns appeared seated on the other side of a wide gate. Bongo drums and acoustic guitars in hand, they were all smiles, and I realized the evening was just getting started. The next few hours, in fact, were a delightful mix of "Franciscan fun" replete with singing, holy joke-telling, vocation testimonies, and, finally, Night Prayer.

That night I had the opportunity to meet some of the sisters. I had the strange sensation that I had known them for a long time . . . or, perhaps, it was as if they had known me. Though they were vowed to a life of poverty and simplicity, I realized immediately that these were amazing and extraordinary women. I also knew instinctively that I would remain close to those sisters for a long time. Indeed, it was so.

A short while later, a small contingent of sisters left San Severino to refound a community in Camerino. The previous community had been forced to leave after the earthquake of 1997 damaged their monastery and church. The Poor Clare monastery of Camerino was also important to the Franciscans of the Marches region because it housed the remains of Camilla Battista Varano, whose canonization was imminent.[2] The sisters—faithful and bold—would return and rebuild. (Little did they know that history would repeat itself, and they would be forced to return after another earthquake in 2016 caused much more damage.)

I soon developed a wonderful relationship with the sisters. It was they who encouraged and supported me to begin bringing pilgrimage groups to the Franciscan places in Italy, which eventually included visits to their monasteries.

So when I initially began accompanying pilgrimage groups to the Franciscan places in Italy, I studied the life of St. Francis thoroughly and earned a certificate in Franciscan studies. I even wrote a book about him, *St. Francis of Assisi: Passion, Poverty, and the Man Who Transformed the Catholic Church*. And as I grew in my knowledge of Francis, it seemed as if Clare was there hidden in the background—silently, mysteriously.

In fact, though I had become well-versed on the life of St. Francis, I always felt a little embarrassed that I did not know much about St. Clare. I wanted to know more. Therefore, I set out to learn about her: I took a course on her life; I read the medieval sources, including her writings and letters, the Legends, and the Acts of Canonization; and I read some of the contemporary biographies.

Yet, as I learned about the life of St. Clare, I realized something: I already knew her. In fact, I had been watching her for many years. Indeed, I realized that in observing the sisters, I had already come to know St. Clare. While in Assisi, I had seen the body of St. Clare countless times, but it was inside the Poor Clare monastery where I saw her face.

Thus, the book you are about to read is more than a biography of a woman who lived eight centuries ago; instead, it is about the St. Clare I have met: I have prayed with her, received consolation from her, bantered and laughed with her, even cried with her. St. Clare is, to me, a mother and a sister and even our daughter, whose name is Claremarie.

The other characters who appear and interact with one another in this book are also real. I have met them in Italy and in the United States in Franciscan friaries, Poor Clare monasteries, and among lay families who follow the spirit of St. Francis in their own homes. Thus, though this book is nominally about St. Clare of Assisi, it is really about relationships.

It is my hope and prayer that this book may become for you a window into the life and spirit of St. Clare—just as I once glimpsed into the enclosure of a Poor Clare monastery some fifteen years ago. And as I was illuminated by what I experienced, may you, too, discover this great woman who is "St. Clare of Assisi, Light from the Cloister."

PROLOGUE: HER NAME SHALL BE "LIGHT"

(1193 Anno Domini)

My dove, my perfect one, is only one, the darling of her mother, flawless to her that bore her.

SONG OF SOLOMON 6:9

EARLY in the morning at dawn, Ortulana was awoken when the first rays of light penetrated the narrow window of her towering castle in upper Assisi. The noblewoman arose and looked out the window to the east, the Orient. The light was just beginning to break through the darkness of the night as the sun arose behind the mountain called Subasio.[3] Her city, then known as Ascesi (Ascending), was home to a son who had risen just ten years earlier.[4] His name was Francis. A daughter was about to rise. And her name would be "light." In time, the great son and daughter of Assisi would dispel the darkness of their city and illuminate lands far, far beyond.

Ortulana stood for a moment at the window, gazing at the great beauty of Umbria. She looked up at the mighty mountain to the southeast and down at the great Spoleto Valley sprawled out before her to the south. She stood there for a moment, taking it all in. It was so stunningly beautiful.

The fortified tower-like castle where she lived was not far from the ruined Roman theater and sepulchral monument.

On the other side of her castle was the city cathedral built over the relics of the city's first bishop and patron, San Rufino. Her mighty palace soared high into the air, rivaling the height of the cathedral's bell tower and façade.[5]

The bells suddenly rang, bringing her back to the moment. Ortulana descended the staircase and walked down the corridor, where her servant greeted her and unbolted the thick door for her. She stood there while she took a deep breath. She exhaled and walked through the door. She was ready.

Ortulana then walked across the square to the cathedral of Assisi, San Rufino. She was filled with eagerness and enthusiasm that morning. The rest of Assisi was abuzz with excitement, too, as practically all its citizens were flocking to the church.

Ortulana was a woman of the highest status in Assisi. She descended from the powerful family of Fiumi and had seven knights in her family. She could trace her lineage all the way back to King Pepin and Charlemagne, the first Holy Roman emperor.[6] Her husband, Favarone, was from the prominent line of Offreduccio. He was a knight, and his family, too, boasted an imperial past. Their family was one of just twenty prominent and respected families that made up Assisi's powerful ruling class—the *Majores* (Majors). As Favarone was the youngest brother of his family, his role was that of the *miles* of the family—the armed knight. As such, he was frequently away from Assisi on knightly pursuits as his position demanded.

Ortulana and Favarone lived together with extended family, including siblings, nieces, and nephews. Favarone's older brother, Monaldo, was the acting head of the family. Such living arrangements were commonplace, especially for people of noble standing. Monaldo and the other men in the family were known for their warlike and irascible tempers.

Her house was one of the largest in Assisi and great sums were spent there.[7] She was the *domina* of her household and, as such, had headship and charge over all the servants and women of the house. Her life was replete with castles in the countryside, guards, servants, and ladies-in-waiting. She had fine jewels and clothing. She frequently attended extravagant festivals, balls, and lavish banquets where there was music and dancing.

Despite the worldly privileges that were hers to enjoy, however, Ortulana never took pleasure in that life. Her name meant "gardener" in the Umbrian lexis, but she was destined to cultivate a garden of a different sort.

She entered into the church joyfully, though she felt a little uneasy. The nave was already full, and people were overflowing outside onto the square. A group of faithful pilgrims was departing that very day, and Ortulana would be one among them. They were headed to Rome and then on to the grotto of St. Michael in Apulia. The liturgical send-off ritual was about to be celebrated by the canon priest of the cathedral. It was always a poignant and moving ceremony.

When pilgrims set forth on the journey, emotion was heavy in the air. Though loved ones shared in the same enthusiasm with their relations who were going away on their journey, they could not hide their sadness . . . or their fear. Prayers in the church offered them a space to gather and say their goodbyes. With grace, the separation would be temporary; hopefully they would safely return.

Pilgrimage during the Middle Ages was, indeed, not without risks. The wayfarers faced the very real threats of disease, robbery, shipwreck, or violence. In fact, often they never returned, as death was too often an unwelcome companion.

The rite began with the pilgrims standing before the priest at the altar. They aligned themselves according to rank: the highest noblemen stood first; they were followed by the middle-class Minors, then the lowlier commoners, while the poorest peasants stood at the end. Their rank in life was reflected by their clothing, which was governed by civil statutes known as sumptuary laws.

The noblemen wore velvet caps, hose with fine overcoats, thick belts, and buckles made of gold. The noblewomen wore garlands or crowns in their hair, ornate robes or flowing gowns fastened at the collar by a round buckle, necklaces, and jewelry. The Minors—including the merchants—wore high-quality garments of the brightest colors. The poor peasants and serfs were dressed simply in leather breeches, with coarse brown tunics made of wool closed at the waist by a heavy belt for attaching working tools.

However, the priest soon gave each pilgrim identical tunics: a gray coarse garment with a cross sown on the front. It was not very different from what the peasants were already wearing. The pilgrims removed their outer clothes and donned the pilgrim's tunic. They were now dressed identically.

Next, they were given a walking staff and a small leather pouch in which they could carry only one day's ration of food. When they exhausted their rations, they would become dependent on Providence. Since their destination was Rome, they were given a small wooden cross with a key attached to it—the symbol of St. Peter and the papacy—which they affixed to their tunics. The garb would set them apart and designate them as pilgrims, while the key would be the sign that they were going to Rome. (Pilgrims going to Compostela in Spain wore a scallop shell, while those going to the Holy Land wore the Jerusalem cross.)

Though Ortulana lived in a world where everyone's identity was based on class, status, and rank—which were essentially inherited through birthright—her faith compelled her to long for something else. Despite her worldly privilege, Ortulana was now dressed identically to the others, including the commoners. They were penitential pilgrims.

Ortulana was a devout and pious Christian woman who had always sought to listen to the voice of the Lord. She was strongly drawn to the devotion of pilgrimage, and she had already been to St. James of Compostela in Spain and even beyond the sea to the Holy Land. Yet, recently, the voice of the Lord told her to go to Rome and the grotto of St. Michael.[8]

While Ortulana was on pilgrimage, she felt closest to the Lord. For her and other pious pilgrims, pilgrimage was the ideal way to live the Christian life. To be a pilgrim meant surrendering the things of the world. The insecurity and instability of pilgrimage would force them to trust completely in God's providence. Further, as a woman of that era, it gave her one of the only opportunities she would ever have to leave the confines of her native city and journey beyond Assisi.

In fact, it was only beyond the city walls of Assisi as a pilgrim where she could fully surrender her earthly titles and possessions and become free to embrace her true identity as a simple child of the heavenly Father. On the road, no one had identity, status, or class; no one owned castles or palaces; no one jockeyed for standing or prestige; there was no intrigue or maneuvering for more power and property. Instead, all depended equally on the providence of God in addition to one another. There, on the road, Ortulana was free to walk simply in the footsteps of Jesus Christ. As a pilgrim, Ortulana possessed nothing other than poverty, which she secretly and quietly yearned for.

The priest concluded the send-off liturgy with the ancient prayer for pilgrims: "O God, you who brought your servant, Abraham, out from the land of Ur of the Chaldeans, protecting him in his wanderings across the desert, we ask that you watch over these pilgrims, your servants, as they walk in the love of your name to St. Peter in Rome and the grotto of St. Michael. And may the blessing of God, Father, Son, and Holy Spirit be with you wherever you may go. Amen."

After the priest gave the final blessing with the relics of San Rufino, the pilgrims said their last prayers and farewells to their loved ones. The townspeople followed them as far as the city walls of Assisi. There, at the southern city gate known as Moiano, the small band of pilgrims left Assisi. As they passed beyond the wall, they looked up at the frescoed images of Sts. Sebastian and Rocco, patrons of pilgrims and those suffering from skin diseases. They paused and made their prayers of intercession that they would be kept safe and healthy.

The pilgrims walked toward the plain below and passed by the Church of St. Anastasio. They then walked past the cluster of homes in Valecchie and the springs of Galletta. The ancient monastery of San Masseo was one road over to their left. When they reached the plain, they turned left and walked south on the road known as the Via Antiqua (ancient road).[9] As they walked, they looked back at Assisi to their left. No one said anything, but they all realized that they had just left what was their "world." Though none could have known it at that moment, they were tracing the same steps that another woman from Assisi would make in just eighteen years when she would leave what was her world.

The pilgrims from Assisi then walked south toward the city of Foligno. From there, they joined what remained of the Via Flaminia—the ancient Roman road that traversed the Italian peninsula from Rome on the Tyrrhenian Sea to the port cities of Fanum and Riminium on the Adriatic.

Ten days later, they arrived in Rome. Ortulana and the other pilgrims recited the ancient creed and paid their homage to Peter. They then spent a few days praying and visiting the other Constantinian basilicas—including the church built over the tomb of St. Paul, as well as those built in honor of St. Mary and St. John. Then the retinue from Assisi continued their pilgrimage south along the ancient Appian Way to southern Italy, where St. Michael the Archangel appeared to a shepherd some seven centuries earlier.

While on pilgrimage, there was plenty of time to reflect on one's life. And Ortulana was thinking about hers. She was happy, but she secretly longed for a more fulfilling and permanent way to live the Christian life.

In Assisi, she lived her religion to the fullest as a married wealthy noblewoman. She faithfully loved her husband and family; she loved God and neighbor; she prayed constantly; she served others in humility, especially the poor. And she frequently gave away what she could to them. Despite her best efforts, though, she secretly longed for something else. She wanted more.

As a young girl, she had thought about entering a monastery. However, her noble heritage would have followed her even there. Even within the monastic cloister, she would have led a privileged life replete with servants and other comforts. She would have spent her time praying the Divine Office in Latin and would have had little time or contact with the poor.

In the end, she followed the dictates of custom and tradition and married the man chosen for her. It was an arranged marriage based on bettering both families' stations. Certainly, she loved her husband and served him willingly and graciously as custom and religious observance required. Yet there was something missing in her heart. That spiritual tug had never left her. And this tug was, in fact, one of the reasons she so often went on pilgrimage.

However, her yearnings notwithstanding, she would always return to Assisi . . . and to that same life of worldly privilege. There had to be a way for her, as a woman, to live the more authentic Christian life she felt called to. She wanted something else, but she did not know what it was. As she walked, she prayed and asked the Lord to show her the way, to show her what to do.

In truth, in that moment, that "way" was closer to her than she could have ever known. Suddenly, Ortulana felt something move deep within her. It was not a physical movement; it was a movement of the Spirit. She stopped walking and closed her eyes. She then smiled broadly.

She told her traveling companion, Pacifica, that she needed to ride in the accompanying carriage. Pacifica was the younger daughter of Guelfuccio, the son of Bernardo, and a relative and neighbor of Ortulana.[10]

Pacifica immediately knew something was wrong. Though Ortulana was from a privileged background and had the means of traveling by horse or carriage, she always walked while on pilgrimage. Jesus walked, the apostles walked, the penitents walked; therefore Ortulana chose to walk. Now, however, she knew she needed to rest.

"Why are you smiling, Ortulana?" asked Pacifica. "It's as if a warm, peaceful light has suddenly come over you. What is it?"

"The Lord just revealed to me that I'm with child!"

"Oh, Ortulana, praise God! We must turn back now and return to Assisi! You need to rest!"

"No, I am still at the beginning of my term. We can still get to St. Michael and be back to Assisi in six weeks' time. The Spirit is telling me that she will need extra graces throughout her life."

"Her? Do you think you are carrying a girl? Do you not want a son?" responded Pacifica.

"No, I am carrying a girl. And I know that she will go far in her life journey: her life will be a great pilgrimage. St. Michael and the angels will bless her. Her life will be like those of the prophets—*a pilgrim and stranger* in this world—and she will serve the Lord in poverty and humility!"[11]

Back in Assisi, as the time of her delivery approached, Ortulana began to feel apprehension. This was her first delivery, and childbirth was dangerous at the time.[12]

She went into the chapel to pray. She knelt and prayed before the crucified Christ for the Lord to bring her safely through the dangers of childbirth. Suddenly, she heard a voice say to her, "Do not be afraid, for you will give birth in safety to a light that will give light more clearly than light itself and shine brilliantly in the world."[13] Ortulana opened her eyes, and immediately a spirit of peace came over her, casting out all anxiety and fear.

In 1194, eight days after her daughter was born, according to custom, Ortulana took her daughter to the baptistery font in the Cathedral of San Rufino.[14] As the priest poured water over her daughter's head, Ortulana gazed into the eyes of her child and knew there was something extraordinary about her.

"I will call her *Clara* (Clare)," Ortulana said. In the Middle Ages, names were important. Names assigned to children were believed to guide and direct the individual as well as those close to them. "Her name shall be 'Light.' I know she will be a light to the world."[15]

Clare took her first steps in Assisi, where she grew up. Ortulana would protect her firstborn daughter and keep particularly close to her. She would instruct her in everything she knew: how to read and write, how to spin yarn and do needlework. Yet the most important thing she would do would be to instruct her daughter in the facets of the Christian life: practicing the virtues; loving God and neighbor; praying, living, and sharing in community; and loving and serving the poor.

In the end, however, Ortulana would be Clare's earthly and spiritual guide for just a short time. After that, it would be the daughter who would become the mother's teacher and guide. And the daughter would teach her mother much greater things.

> *A tree is known by its fruit and the fruit is recommended by its tree. The richness of the divine generosity preceded in the root, so that an abundance of holiness would follow in the branch.*
>
> LEGEND 1:2

1

WAR AND EXILE

(1198 Anno Domini)

I slept, but my heart was awake. Hark! my beloved is knocking. "Open to me, my sister, my love, my dove, my perfect one."

Song of Solomon 5:2

IT was spring 1198. Ortulana was working diligently at household chores in the women's common room upstairs. Her servants were with her as well as her neighbors, Pacifica and Bona. Clare and her two younger sisters, Catherine and Beatrice, were there, too.[16] Though their noble station and rank in life dictated that servants alone do manual labor, Ortulana worked alongside them. As they worked together, they were full of joy and spirit.

Suddenly, Ortulana's brother-in-law, Clare's uncle Monaldo, burst through the door. He appeared terrified as he shouted, "The emperor is dead! Henry VI just died! We're finished!" Ortulana became alarmed and immediately started reciting prayers along with the other women. Clare's sisters sensed the tension and started crying.

Though Clare was only five years old, she understood things far beyond her age and she knew what might happen as a result of the young emperor's untimely death. The

Majors of Assisi were aligned with the German emperor, whose empire extended into northern Italy as far south as Umbria. But he was now deceased. And his successor was his son, a mere child of three. With a power vacuum in Germany, Assisi would lose imperial protection, rendering the city vulnerable to attack.

Indeed, Conrad of Urslingen, the count who ruled over Assisi on behalf of the emperor through the duchy of Spoleto, promptly abandoned the Rocca fortress that stood guard over the city. He quietly returned to Spoleto, leaving the Majors to fend for themselves. Previously, no one would have dared lift a finger against the fortress, for that would have incurred the wrath of the mighty emperor. But now there was no emperor, just a powerless toddler with a powerful title.

Clare's family worried who might assert themselves and try to take over Assisi. Some of the disenfranchised citizenry of Assisi, particularly the Minors, could use this as an opportunity to rebel. Or Perugia—Assisi's perennial enemy—might seize the moment and attack. Or the pope himself could assert his authority and try to annex Assisi into the papal territories, which were already strong in Umbria. Favarone's family and the other Majors now faced exile . . . or worse. Clare, too, began to pray.

The fears of the Majors were soon realized. Clare was in the family chapel praying when she heard the ruckus: "It's the Minors! The Minors are coming!" her uncle shouted as he ran through the house. "Everyone, change your clothes! Quickly!" he commanded.

Clare's mother dashed into the chapel and snatched her and her sisters. Ortulana was already wearing servant's clothes, and she threw a simple tunic over the girls' noble dresses. As Ortulana rushed her daughters down the stairs, Clare caught a glimpse of the scene outside the window. She was alarmed at the sight of men charging up the hill past their house and the cathedral. Armed with swords and spears, as well as sticks and clubs, they were racing up toward the Rocca fortress.

The family inconspicuously slipped out of the house through the servant's entrance and made their way up past the old ruined Roman theater, amphitheater, and the mausoleum. Finally they reached a small castle well up on Mount Subasio. It was one of the castles owned by Clare's father. They would be safe there for the time being.[17]

From the safety of the little fortress atop Mount Subasio, Clare's family watched in horror as the Minors razed the Rocca Maggiore. They dismantled the stones of the castle one by one. The destruction continued by torchlight throughout the night and into the next day. The Minors then began using the stones from the Rocca fortress to reinforce the city walls for protection against reprisals from the Majors.

The Minors hated the Rocca fortress. For them, it symbolized the feudal way of life and unjust rule over them. From that castle, the city's rulers levied taxes against them, passed laws that supported the Majors, and otherwise harassed and intimidated them.

The Minors promptly swore allegiance to Assisi and promised they would do everything within their powers to defend it. They wrote a new charter of liberty and voted in a city mayor, called a *podestà,* in addition to new city consuls. Assisi was now a republic free of feudalistic rule.

It was called a *commune*—a municipality or city-state—named after them, the commoners.

The new government building was established on the square of the main marketplace in the center of town where the common people lived. From there, they would work to defend their newfound freedoms by planning for defense and war and writing new charters and statutes. It would now be for the Minors to decide the fate of Assisi.

Over the following days and weeks, some of the Majors stayed in Assisi and pledged allegiance to the new government in collaboration with the Minors. Clare's family, however, preferred to wait and see if there could be a compromise. But their strategy did not fare well, as the wrath of the Minors would periodically explode, leading them to tear down one noble castle after another. Clare's family palace, in fact, though next to the cathedral, was not spared and suffered a vicious attack one afternoon.

Soon the Minors directed their reprisals outside of the center of Assisi, and they set their sights on the castles atop Mount Subasio. One evening, they rushed up and attacked the castle of Leonardo of Gislerio in Sasso Rosso. The noble castellan had sworn enmity against the new city-state and had taken refuge with his family there in his fortress. They barely got out alive before his castle was destroyed. His young daughter, Filippa, was there in the mayhem. Perhaps she met Clare during those days and recalled her peaceful presence many years later when she decided to follow her at San Damiano as one of her first followers.

After the attack on Sasso Rosso, Clare's father and uncles knew the Majors had no place in the new republican government. It was not safe for them to stay in Assisi. Thus, they began preparing for exile.

All the while, what was a tragedy for Clare's family and the other Majors was cause for rejoicing for the Minors. Among that furious and violent mix of Minors, soldiers, artisans, and ruffians was a young seventeen-year-old son of a Minor cloth merchant. He, too, celebrated victory together with his brother and father. It would still be seven years, however, before Francis's thirst for worldly glory would be transformed by grace into spiritual glory.[18]

. . .

In the year 1200, Clare's family left Assisi for Perugia, where they were taken in by relatives. Clare lived with a distant cousin, a girl her same age, named Benvenuta (which means "welcome"). Like Filippa, she, too, would one day follow Clare as one of her first companions.[19]

In Perugia, rancor was heavy in the air. The men in Clare's family constantly brooded over their woes and plotted their return to Assisi. There was incessant talk of loss and partisan chatter of retribution and vendetta.

After two years, in November 1202, Clare's father ran through the Perugia house yelling triumphantly, "We were victorious today! The Minors tried to attack Perugia this morning, but the Perugian troops and our men ambushed them while they attempted to cross the Tiber River! Our own Monaldo fought courageously with them! It was a total rout! What a glorious day today is! We'll be back in Assisi soon!"[20] Favarone rushed back down the stairs with his brothers and cousins to revel in the streets below. There was dancing and elation throughout Perugia as the entire city rejoiced.

Clare stayed inside with her mother and relatives. Instead of celebrating, however, they went to the chapel to pray. Clare felt compassion for the dead, their families, the wounded, and the imprisoned. She also felt sorrow that members of her family were jubilant despite the suffering of others.

Suddenly, the tone of those reveling outside changed. Instead of celebrating triumphantly, the townspeople were now screaming and jeering. Clare rushed to the window with the other women and looked down at the streets below. She was horrified at what she saw.

The city consuls and priors entered victoriously on their warhorses through the city walls, built millennia earlier by the Etruscans, at the southern Marzian Gate. Their banners and heralds—displaying the symbol of the city, the griffin—were held up gloriously on high. That warlike mythological creature with the body of a lion and head and wings of an eagle represented Perugia well. With its menacing beak and talons ready to strike, it was the perfect symbol for Perugia's warlike spirit. According to local lore, the Perugians had once captured and killed a griffin on a nearby mountain.

The Perugian soldiers followed them, pulling the bloody Assisian prisoners of battle. Clare looked on with dread at the prisoners who were chained pathetically in iron collars and paraded like farm animals. Some were stripped and nearly naked. The sadistic guards took delight in beating and harassing their pitiful captives. They smiled as they kicked and flogged them mercilessly with knotted ropes. From the windows and balconies of their homes, residents urged them on and threw scraps of food and excrement down at the prisoners.

When the pitiful procession reached the central square with its grand fountain, the city's captain and notaries looked on approvingly from the balconies of their palaces. Even the bishop, from his illustrious residence adjacent to the cathedral (known as the *Canonica*), stepped out onto his marble balcony. Pope Innocent III had been his guest there just a few years earlier in 1198 to dedicate the cathedral to St. Lawrence. The bishop, too, assessed the situation and nodded favorably.

As the gruesome spectacle arrived near the tower-like house where Clare's family was residing, the future saint instinctively ran down the stairs into the kitchen and snatched up some bread and a jug of water. Dodging the ladies-in-waiting who tried to stop her, she raced out to the street. She jostled her way through the crowd of jeering Perugians and exiled Assisians and ran toward the line of prisoners with her aid. Before getting close enough, however, she was snatched up forcefully by a brute of a man. She looked up to see the ruddy face of her irate uncle.

"Get back in that house, Clare, right now!" Monaldo barked at her. Grabbing her by the back of her cloak, he lifted her up off the ground like a rag doll and tossed her in the direction of their home. He then turned his attention back to the prisoners and continued humiliating them.

As Clare returned home dejectedly, she looked back at the prisoners as they continued their pathetic march toward the city dungeon. Despite the wretchedness of their condition, one prisoner stood out and seemed different from the others. He had an aura about him, and despite his suffering, his demeanor seemed optimistic, even joyful.[21]

Clare was struck by this man and watched him. Just as he reached the dungeon door, Monaldo landed a punishing kick on his backside, sending him tumbling through the dark door. He then yelled at him, "Get in there, knight-boy! Enjoy the glories of knighthood now!"

His name was Francis. But it would be another four years before he would put down his sword for the last time, and ten before she would renounce everything to follow him.[22]

Hardly had she been brought into the light, than the little Clare began to shine sufficiently in the darkness of the world and to be resplendent in her tender years through the propriety of her conduct. . . . She freely stretched out her hand to the poor and satisfied the needs of many out of the abundance of her house. In order that her sacrifice would be more pleasing to God, she would deprive her own body of delicate foods and, sending them secretly through intermediaries, she would nourish the bodies of the poor.

LEGEND 2:3

2

BACK TO ASSISI

What is that coming up from the wilderness, like a column of smoke, perfumed with myrrh and frankincense, with all the fragrant powders of the merchant?

Song of Solomon 3:6

IN 1205, the Majors were finally able to negotiate the end of their exile and return to Assisi. And there, on the same land adjacent to the Cathedral of San Rufino, Clare's family set out to rebuild their fortified home . . . and their fortune.

As their first objective was defense, they rebuilt their fortified castle next to the cathedral. As knights, the men were well-versed in the art of warfare and military strategy, and they knew how to use their weapons. They had to be ready for war, as another attack against them or Assisi could come without warning, so they trained frequently for battle in tournaments and jousts. They also sometimes joined the ranks of other allied cities when called upon to defend their territories, too.

When training or in battle, they wore armor consisting of cloth or heavy plate mail. Shields, long and short swords, clubs, spears, lances, pikes, halberds, and crossbows were common accessories. Throughout Clare's childhood, visitors with swords or daggers on their hip often came to discuss military strategies and consult for city defense.

Next, the men of Favarone's family set to work looking for ways to improve the family fortune. Important and influential men came and went: the *podestà*, city consuls, and magistrates came, as did merchants, heads of guilds, and leaders of the local confraternities. Important land deals were negotiated, business matters hammered out, and political machinations plotted.

As a result of their ambition and industriousness, their fiefs grew larger. They possessed olive groves, timber forests, hunting grounds, streams, and wells. They owned lands in the countryside with castles, pastures, and mills. They earned money by charging rents and exacting payments for the use of their properties. In their leisure, they enjoyed banquets where they feasted and drank, or they entertained themselves in contests of archery, hammer-throwing, hunting, jousting, and hawking.

Outside Clare's house, there was constant activity as well. From its important position in upper Assisi next to the cathedral, there was always clamor and activity to be seen in the square below. The town criers and heralds shouted out proclamations and directives. Knights and crusaders trotted by on horseback on their way to or from the Holy Land. Pilgrims and penitents ambled by, begging alms and talking about religion. Merchants and vendors hawked their wares. Peasants led donkeys with carts full of produce. On important feast days, the bishop and canons led processions into the cathedral. All the while, beggars and the lame cursed at those with better fortune, while the insane shouted at real or imaginary companions.

Most well-to-do young women had plenty of idle time and would frequently observe the action by constantly rushing to the windows or the balcony to watch. This was the appropriate place for an unmarried young woman to see or be seen.

The noblewomen of Assisi enjoyed the privileges of luxury and comfort in their large palaces and castles. Women of Clare's status wore garments made of silk and satin hemmed with gold or silver. They avoided working with their hands, which was frowned upon socially or even forbidden by custom. Instead, manual labor was given to those of lower rank—the servants and ladies-in-waiting.

Noblewomen of that era had access to books and some education provided by relatives or in-house tutors. They knew how to play musical instruments like the lute and the lyre. But with no housework or manual labor to do, most of their leisure time was spent organizing and attending social events. There were always lavish banquets, festivals, balls, feasts, or other merriments to frequent.

Young damsels of marriageable age were chaperoned to social events. There they danced to music and amused themselves, listening to romantic ballads sung in old French by traveling troubadours and minstrels. They delighted in the entertainments provided by the wandering jongleurs or Assisi's own *tripudianti.* In the springtime, under close supervision, they wore their finest garments for the celebrated *Calendimaggio* festival as they gawked and giggled at brawny horsemen who showed off their riding skills and talents.

Women of all ages made sure they were kept abreast of the gossip and dirty secrets of other families. They frequently engaged in idle chatter where they spread rumors and gloated over the misfortune of others. At the same time, they did their best to ensure that their own family's reputation was held in high esteem and not tarnished.

Yet Clare and the women of her household rarely took part in vain pursuits. Instead, from a very young age, Clare learned to "veil" herself from worldly affairs by closing herself off and exercising the hidden virtues of modesty and prayer. With her mother, sisters, and the other women in her home, Clare lived what was her first experience of community. Lady Bona later testified about Clare's childhood, "She always stayed in the house, hidden, not wanting to be seen by those who passed in front of her house."[23]

And it was there within that house that something mysterious took place. Despite the vanity of the world around her, grace was abounding and increasing, quietly but powerfully, within the soul of this very young girl. Like Mary, the Mother of God, she was given many treasures and graces, which she received and pondered in her heart. What she was learning as a young girl was something she would do for the rest of her life: she was taking custody of and preciously guarding the gifts God was bestowing upon her. In this, she became like a "tabernacle of the Lord."

The how or why of it will remain forever a mystery. Clare demonstrated such a remarkable disposition toward holiness and seemed to cooperate with God's grace so naturally that some did believe, in fact, that, almost like another Mary, she had been "sanctified in her mother's womb."[24]

It is clear, in any case, that the soil in which the sower sowed his seeds was clear of thorns and rocky ground; instead, it was fertile (see Mt 13:1–9). And this was due, without a doubt, to those who were close to her.

Clare's mother, Ortulana—the gardener—was a holy woman and had, no doubt, the greatest influence on Clare's spiritual life.[25] She and the other women of Clare's household were less focused on the restoration of the family's worldly fortunes—"storing up treasures on earth"—and instead were more concerned with spiritual fortunes—storing up "treasures in heaven, where neither moth nor rust consumes and where thieves do not break in and steal" (Mt 6:19–20). In this, she indeed planted a fertile orchard in her daughter.

Thus, as an adolescent, Clare adopted the ways of her mother and prayed constantly, spurned soft clothing, and wore a rough woolen hair shirt made of horsehair directly on her skin for penance and asceticism. She always spoke of the things of God.[26] Like her mother, she, too, engaged in manual labor, such as cleaning and washing, though it was against custom and there were household servants whose job it was to do such work.[27] Thus, Clare practiced the holy life from the time she was a young girl.

And that holiness involved her affinity for the poor. The first witness in her canonization process testified that "Clare very much loved the poor."[28] She would often send food or other alms to the poor. They never had to go far to deliver it, as the poor were everywhere: the crippled, diseased, maimed, and disfigured. In the past, when cities were smaller and most people lived in the countryside, poverty was not as widespread; people were cared for by their families and the community. However, since the rise of the marketplaces inside the cities, urban poverty had now become a veritable scourge.

It was easy to become poor and lose everything in that era. It only took a calamity such as a bad fall, a serious illness, a fire in one's shop or home, or a bad harvest. The city municipality did not provide much aid for the poor; there were just a few hospitals for the lepers (known as *leprosaria*) well outside the city walls down in the valley. The institutions of the Church—aside from some pious individuals or small communities—were not then adequately equipped to do much either. Therefore, they wandered around the streets or lay in the alleyways, sometimes even near death. At times, the town guards would cast them out of the city. Then they would crowd around the city gates, begging alms or money from all those who came or went.

When Clare came face to face with the poor, she was deeply moved. She would gaze into their eyes, where she saw their pain and suffering. It was not difficult for her to love them: she was already in love with Someone who had once suffered the greatest Passion. Therefore, when she was close to the poor and suffering, she felt close to Christ himself.[29]

Clare soon became well-known throughout Assisi for her holiness, and the townspeople began to hold her in great esteem because of her good manner of life.[30] Later, when she was being canonized, the household watchman summarized what people thought of her: "Although she lived in a privileged household full of great wealth, she nevertheless saved the food they were given to eat, put it aside, and gave it to the poor. While she was still in her father's house, she wore a rough garment under her other clothes. . . . She fasted, prayed, and did other pious deeds, . . . and she had been inspired by the Holy Spirit from the beginning."[31]

As Clare grew in piety, however, a rift began to grow between the holiness she was striving to live and the lordly worldly powers around her. And it would not take long before this paradox in Clare's life would develop into a full-scale conflict that eventually would prove irreconcilable.

Indeed, while some were discerning how Clare was growing in virtue, others noticed instead how she was growing in beauty. She was tall, with fair skin, long, blonde hair, and blue eyes. Locals in Assisi referred to her as the "silver dove" and said she had a "beautiful face."[32] She was becoming a beautiful young woman.

Though Clare strove to keep this beauty of hers hidden from the world, she could not keep it from the men in her household. And it seemed they had one thing on their minds: the enlargement of their family's privilege, power, and status. And there was one sure way to do it.

Clare frequently overheard the men discussing her future as well as that of her sisters and cousins. There was persistent speculation and intrigue about potential alliances with other noble families of Assisi, Umbria, and even beyond. Ultimately, they were concerned with one question and one question alone: which marriage would make their family stronger and more powerful?

Over supper one evening, Clare's uncle, Monaldo, talked with her father. Dinners in noble households were lavish affairs. Clare's family was privileged with wait staff and servants who brought copious amounts of spiced meat and game with sauced vegetables on precious platters along with fine wines in goblets.

"Favarone," Monaldo said as he gulped down his wine, "your daughter has a lot of potential: she is intelligent and bright in addition to being a real beauty. She will do great things for this family . . ."

He then turned to Clare, saying to her directly, "If you think you enjoy the privileges and wealth of this household here, just wait . . . You're going to be really rich one day! You will surely marry a great nobleman. He will be a count, a marquis, or even a duke. You could even become a princess!"[33]

As he said this, her uncle nonetheless noticed how Clare ate very little, as she often abstained from meals.[34] He often remonstrated with his brother about this. "Favarone, your daughter hardly eats a morsel! She's so thin and always seems sickly. And she talks only of religion. She needs to be healthy and strong! One day she will bring great privileges to this family!"

Clare was used to their conversations as she had heard them as long as she could remember. But she tried not to pay much attention to them. *Yes, I will one day be rich*, Clare thought to herself as she took some meat from her plate and hid it under her garments to later give to the poor. *I will one day be a princess. I will be the richest and most privileged woman! I will indeed marry a nobleman. But he will be the Most Noble Spouse!*

Ortulana gazed over at her daughter with a comforting and reassuring glance. She knew the desires of Clare's heart and the struggles she internalized. Ortulana had a deep and abiding faith in the Lord. Like Monaldo, Ortulana believed that Clare would bring great privileges to the family. But she knew that they would be privileges of a different kind.

On August 11 each year, a High Mass was celebrated for the feast of Assisi's patron saint, San Rufino, in the cathedral.[35] It began with a great procession that paraded into the cathedral from the square below Clare's home. Clare sometimes permitted herself to watch it from the window of her home, as the procession was an exercise in piety and she had a strong devotion to San Rufino, the protector of Assisi. However, it often left her with a feeling of sadness.

The procession was a grandiose and ornate display rich in spectacle and pageantry. The townspeople processed according to rank and importance; they were ordered from the least to the greatest. It began with the Minors who wore velvet caps and long colorful cloaks denoting their well-to-do status. Next were the noble ladies of the court wearing flowing colored gowns and jewels; their children, carrying flowers, were also vested in fine garments with crowns and headdresses. Then came the Majors and other noblemen who had returned to power: Clare's father, uncles, and cousins were always there dressed in full regalia. After them came armored knights and crusaders riding gallantly on horseback in full armor.

Finally, in the end, the trumpeters, drummers, and flag bearers concluded the procession, carrying the standard of the Assisi quarter of San Rufino. They were announcing the arrival of the relics of San Rufino pulled by white oxen draped with the caparison in Assisi's colors of red and blue. The carriage was led by the bishop himself, flanked by cathedral canons. As the bishop passed by with the relics of San Rufino, the lay faithful kneeled down obsequiously to receive his blessing.

As Clare watched the most important personages of Assisi pass by, something seemed to be missing. By now, her spirituality had deepened, and something seemed awry. She was thinking of the words of the Lord who said, "But many that are first will be last, and the last first" (Mt 19:30).

Clare removed herself from the window and went to the household chapel to pray. There she placed herself in front of the crucifix. Only before the cross could she find true consolation. For on the cross, Clare witnessed the God who lowered himself and came down. He was humble, poor, broken, and meek.[36]

There on the cross was God almighty, whom "the highest heaven cannot contain" (cf. 1 Kgs 8:27). There on the cross God humbled himself by taking on human flesh. There on the cross God assumed our sin onto himself. There on the cross was poverty incarnate.

In gazing upon the cross, Clare saw how Christ was poor. She would one day write, "O blessed poverty, who bestows eternal riches on those who love and embrace her! O holy poverty, to those who possess and desire you God promises the kingdom of heaven and offers, indeed, eternal glory and blessed life! O God-centered poverty, whom the Lord Jesus Christ who ruled and now rules heaven and earth, who spoke and things were made, condescended to embrace before all else!"[37]

As Clare gazed up at the crucifix, she asked herself where the poor, crucified Jesus was in the world. The God of the cross seemed so remote from the world she was living in. There, where Clare lived, men were striving to go up, up, up: always more gain, more power, more status, more privileges, more possessions. . . . And this seemed true not only in the world but also—to Clare's sorrow—in the Church.

However, there, on the cross, the Word, the Second Person of the Trinity, lowered himself by going down, down, down. While meditating on the cross, Clare understood something about God. Christ, the Word, had lowered himself into the world. He through whom all things were made became man. Christ was lesser: he was "minor." However, Christ was quite different from the Minors of Assisi who were seeking to go "up."

The paradox Clare was discerning sometimes seemed too much for her to bear. How could she ever reconcile the world she was living in? The world—with its power, servants, pomp, privilege, and all the trappings of comfort and ease proper to her noble station in life—was so different from the other path shown to her through the faith of her mother: prayer, penance, and service to the poor and marginalized. It was as if her feet were in two separate worlds: one in the worldly domain of noble power and privilege, the other in the spiritual realm of prayer and service to the poor.

Clare knew personally what it took to defend the possessions and privileges her family enjoyed: thick walls, bolted doors, tribunals, and even arms. Though she was young, she had personally experienced the tragedy of civil war and exile and all the resulting turmoil and heartache. She had witnessed firsthand the reality of fighting between classes for power.

But she also knew what it felt like to unlock those doors and freely give away what others were fighting so intensely to keep or earn for themselves. She had tasted the freedom and joy that comes from giving rather than receiving. And in her heart, she yearned for more. She longed to give everything away and follow Christ totally and wholly as his and his alone. She desired in her heart to be with her Lord and God. But where? How?

By now, Clare was aware of the longing she had to receive the tonsure and take the veil. That desire in her heart had been there for a long time. But she did not feel drawn to one of the Benedictine monasteries for women—the main option for religious life for women at that time. Clare had visited the Benedictine nuns of Sant'Apollinare and San Paolo of the Abbesses. Yet she was struck by the worldly way of life of the nuns. The feudal way of life that was still alive in the world was deeply ingrained in the cloister. Clare's noble status, in fact, would have followed her even into the monastery.

Most of the men's and women's monasteries were largely feudal institutions ruled over by powerful abbots or abbesses. The noblewomen entered the monastery with their titles, dowries, and even servants, which they kept throughout their lives. They spent most of their time in the choir praying. The commoners or women from "lowborn" families, on the other hand, performed most of the manual labor required within the monastery. The two groups ate, prayed, and slept in separate quarters, and there was little interaction between them. If Clare were to enter a convent, her noble status would place her as a choir nun in the privileged place even within the monastery.

Clare returned to the window and watched the end of the procession as the bishop entered the cathedral. As he went inside, many of the lay faithful followed him in. When Mass began, the heavy wooden door was shut. She then looked back toward the square and watched as the rest of the crowds went home. In a short time, almost everyone was gone. There remained only the lame, the crippled, the sick, and the beggars. Her heart went out to them.

She went back to the chapel to pray and gazed up again at the crucifix. There was something deep in her heart yearning and burning. Clare wanted to imitate Christ, to give away what was hers and become something less. She wanted to become "lesser"—a true "minor."

She knew that she was called to something unique, to a new way of life. She began to feel strongly that she had to do something different with her life. She wanted more than anything else to be with her Lord, to be where he was. But she did not know how or where.

She prayed that God would show her the way, "Lord, what do you want from me? How do you want me to serve you?" she asked as she prayed silently and deeply. She usually felt much consolation in her prayer, and Christ always revealed himself close to her. However, as she listened, she heard and felt nothing. God seemed so far away and she felt desolation within.

Clare sighed as she asked herself, *What is God's will for my life? What is my way?*

Though she felt nothing, in reality, God's way for her was not far off. Indeed, the answer to her prayer was close, so very close.

A short time later, Clare was busy at her household chores ruminating over these things in her heart when she overheard one of the servants excitedly tell her mother, "He's coming! He's coming to San Rufino to preach tomorrow!"

"Who is?" Clare interjected.

"Francis!"

Thus from her infancy, as mercy was growing with her, she bore a compassionate attitude, merciful toward the miseries of the destitute. She held the pursuit of holy prayer as a friend and after she was frequently sprinkled with its holy fragrance, she gradually entered a celibate life. When she did not have a chaplet with which to count the Our Father, she would count her little prayers of the Lord with a pile of pebbles. When she began to feel the first stirrings of holy love, she judged that the passing scene of worldly pride should be condemned, being taught by the unction of the Spirit to place a worthless price upon worthless things. Under her costly and soft clothes, she wore a hair-shirt, blossoming externally to the world, inwardly putting on Christ. Finally, when her family desired that she be married in a noble way, she would in no way consent, but, feigning that she would marry a mortal at a later date, she entrusted her virginity to the Lord.

LEGEND 2:3

3

FRANCIS

Behold, he comes, leaping upon the mountains, bounding over the hills.

SONG OF SOLOMON 2:8

EVERYONE in Assisi knew of Francis. His name was constantly on people's lips in a town that liked to gossip and loved to overhear all manner of tales. Clare knew his story, too, as he was often discussed among work in the common area. While sewing or hemming, preparing meals or cleaning, the women and servants in Clare's household also talked about Francis of Assisi, though more piously.

Clare knew that he was the son of a wealthy cloth merchant, that he had been one of the most promising young men of Assisi, that his youth was spent in affluence, luxury, and ease, that he had fought on the battlefield, that he had been imprisoned in Perugia, that he set out to fight in the Crusades, and that he turned back in Spoleto.

But this same man now embraced a life of prayer, poverty, and penance. His movement, which began with just a few companions—Bernard, Peter, and Giles—was growing rapidly and now numbered many. But they were all men. And this was something Francis hoped would soon change. In fact, he knew it would, for he had received a prophecy.

In 1206, when Francis was still a solitary hermit serving lepers and rebuilding churches around Assisi by himself, the young penitent heard a voice. It took place while he was working on the restoration of a little country church called San Damiano. This was the same place where one year earlier he heard another voice spoken through the crucifix: "Francis, rebuild my House, which as you can see has totally fallen into ruin."[38]

This time it was a prophecy he heard in San Damiano. While Francis was on the roof repairing tiles with the poor and destitute of Assisi who helped him, the Spirit suddenly stirred within him. Francis paused from his work, closed his eyes, and remained motionless for several moments. And the Lord spoke again.

After a moment, he opened his eyes and smiled joyfully. From the roof of San Damiano, Francis shouted out in French to his collaborators and others who happened to be nearby what had just been revealed to him: "Come and help me build the monastery of San Damiano, because holy virgins of Christ will dwell here who will glorify our heavenly Father throughout his holy Church by their celebrated and holy manner of life."[39]

And now the prophecy was nearing its fulfillment: she would soon come.

Many in Assisi and beyond now respected Francis. But not everyone shared the same esteem for the "penitent from Assisi."

"Fanatics!" Clare's uncle roared as he slammed his fist down at the dinner table one evening, startling Clare and her sisters. Monaldo was enraged at the news he had just learned. His younger brother, Scipione, had a son who was destined to be a noble knight like the other men in the household. However, the young man in question, Clare's first cousin Rufino, had other plans. He was now following Francis.

Monaldo shook his head slowly and sighed loudly. He, too, had heard of the "penitents from Assisi" as they were called then.

"They freely give away what they own to live like paupers. They dress in the tunics of peasants. They do manual labor in exchange for alms. They sleep in animal sheds or near ruined churches. And they refuse to accept or touch money!" grumbled Monaldo. As he spoke, he glared at his brother, Scipione, who slumped pitifully and dejectedly in his chair.

Shaking his head, he continued, "Worst of all, they associate with lepers! Will you please tell me what kind of man their leader, Francis, is? He was born rich, but chose to become poor! Who does such a thing? How is it that someone from *our* family has decided to join someone like that?"

Clare's father, however, thought even worse of Francis. "I agree, Brother, that this Francis and the others are fanatics," he said to Monaldo. Turning to his forlorn brother, Scipione, however, he said, "But to me, they are worse than that. We are Christians and religion is important, but fanaticism leads to dangerous sects. You watch . . . I believe they are headed down the same path as that heretic, Valdès of Lyons, France. He, too, was once a wealthy merchant who turned into a penitent. But look at his followers now: they are hiding out in the Alps, excommunicated from the

Church![40] Do everything you can to get your son away from that heretic, Francis!"

"True, but worse than the heretics are the Minors! And their 'founder' is a Minor!" interjected Monaldo. Even though the Majors of Assisi had attempted to make peace with the Minors, there was still plenty of animosity and rancor between them.

Turning toward Scipione, he said, "Your son—a nobleman, a highborn nobleman—is following him, a lesser, a Minor! What a sad day it is for our house. These Minors—these commoners—are burghers! They are uncouth and have no culture. They are utter ignoramuses!" Monaldo scoffed.

"Sure, they're good with numbers and can balance their ledgers," he continued. "But not one of them is cultured, not one of them knows good Latin. Greatness has always come from our class, the nobility." He paused as he shook his head slowly.

"Practically all popes, cardinals, bishops, and abbots come from among our class . . . and most priests, too," he continued. "You cannot bring the Minors up to our level; they will only bring us down to theirs. They have already destroyed Assisi. Mark my words: they will destroy the Church as well!"

After another pause, he glared at his brother, adding, "I tell you, the only thing worse than a wealthy Minor choosing to be poor is a wealthy Major choosing to become poor!" He shook his head again. At this, Clare and her mother exchanged concerned glances.

"Scipione," said Monaldo, again turning to his younger brother. "Do not misunderstand me. I favor religion. However, religion should be decorous and dignifying. If your son really wants to take vows and enter religion, have him do something respectable and become a Benedictine monk. He can join the monks of San Benedetto up on Mount Subasio. Or have him enter San Pietro down by the 'hill of hell.' The abbots of both monasteries are business acquaintances of mine and personal friends. They will accept him. There he will live a life of prayer and ease as a *chorista*. He will never have to stoop and do any manual work. If he stays with Francis and those ragamuffins, he will surely live a life of squalor and destitution beyond your imagination." Scipione wasn't listening; he was in shock at what was happening to him and his family.

While the men spoke disparagingly of Francis, Clare remained quiet and kept her thoughts to herself. Unlike the men in her house, his way of life fired her imagination and spirit. There was something about Francis's story that spoke to Clare. She was intrigued by him. She loved that he had grown up wealthy but gave everything away, that he loved the poor, and the way in which he radiated joy.

In this, Clare was different from most of her peers. She lived during the height of the culture of chivalry and courtesy. Most girls Clare's age giggled as they listened to love stories told of Isolde and Tristan or Guinevere and Lancelot. They were charmed by the tales of brave cavaliers who freed damsels from villains or the heroic crusaders who defended Jerusalem against the Saracens. They watched and swooned over chivalrous knights who jousted or fought hand to hand in tournaments.

Clare, however, was not interested in those tales or spectacles. Instead, she was drawn to the other "genre" of stories told then—the pious, sacred ones—so often read or recounted in the Middle Ages: the legends of the saints. Clare grew up, first and foremost, hearing about St. Rufinus (San Rufino)—the patron of Assisi who had established Assisi's Christian community some thousand years earlier.

According to the legends, Rufino had come from the East to evangelize in Assisi. But the local pagan authorities objected, and he was arrested and tortured. When he persisted in evangelizing, weights were chained to his neck and he was thrown into the Chiascio River nearby. His remains were recovered by the local Christians and later brought inside the city walls of Assisi. Now they were housed in the cathedral, next to Clare's home.

And now it seemed to Clare that another saint was walking once again in the streets of Assisi.

When Clare heard how Francis put down his sword and left his aspirations for knighthood, choosing instead to give away everything in order to embrace the leper and follow Christ in poverty, she thought of the holy ones who were venerated in her time.

To Clare, Francis was like a modern-day St. Anthony of the Desert. Anthony, too, was inspired by the Gospel of Matthew to give away his lands and property to the poor, to flee to the desert, to live the ascetic life: "If you would be perfect, go, sell what you possess and give to the poor, and you will have treasure in heaven" (Mt 19:21).

Or maybe he was a new St. Martin of Tours. Once a soldier in the Roman army some eight centuries earlier, like Francis, he came to find the military life incompatible with his Christian life. And just as Francis embraced lepers and mendicants, Martin of Tours, moved by piety, legendarily cut his military mantle in two with his sword and gave half to a freezing beggar.

Or perhaps he was a St. Bruno, who gave everything away to follow God in the monastery and founded the Carthusian Order. Or maybe he was an Alberic of Citeaux, a Robert of Molesme, or a Bernard of Clairvaux—the Cistercian monks who had recently reformed the Benedictine Order through poverty and diligent work.

Francis indeed was walking in the footsteps of the holy ones. And Clare wanted to hear him. She had her chance when, together with Brother Philip Longo, Francis was invited by the bishop of Assisi, Guido, to preach in the cathedral. When it came time, Clare, accompanied by Bona, slipped out of the house quietly and went to San Rufino. Together Clare and Bona took their places in the back of the cathedral.

In a sermon that was direct and succinct, Francis preached on the poverty of Christ and the Incarnation. He used language that was simple and popular. There were no theological abstractions, and everyone could understand him, even the poor peasants who had also come to listen.[41]

Francis began, "Our Savior loves us so much that he comes down to us where we are. We see how he emptied himself of the divine glories of heaven. Scripture says, 'He humbled himself' as when the 'all-powerful word leaped from heaven, from the royal throne,' into the womb of the Virgin. Yet daily he still comes to us in a humble form; daily he comes down from the 'bosom of the Father' upon the altar in the hands of the priest. Daily he makes himself into bread and wine for us. For love of us."[42] Clare was moved as she listened attentively.

Francis continued, "Who are we that the God of the universe gazes down at us and moves down to be with humanity—his creation—because of love? Who are we that Christ should come into the world born to poor parents, Joseph and Mary? Who are we that Jesus should associate with the marginalized—lepers, tax collectors, and outcasts? Who are we that Our Lord should go to the cross and die on the cross? Who are we that the Lord should assume our sins? We are nothing but poor sinners who are called to go to him and imitate him in poverty and penance." Clare listened intently to every word he said.

"Not long ago, in the Church of St. Mary of the Angels down in the valley, where the brothers and I live now, I heard a Scripture reading from Matthew: 'Take no gold, nor silver, nor copper in your belts, no bag for your journey, nor two tunics, nor sandals, nor a staff.' When I heard that Gospel, I knew poverty was what I wanted; I desired it with all my heart. In that moment, I gave everything I had left and embraced total poverty." Clare imagined that Francis was speaking directly to her.

He continued, "But I soon realized that poverty was not just for me, and God gave me brothers. Together with Bernard and Peter, the first friars, Scripture showed each of us how we were to follow Christ. The Word of God told us that to be 'perfect' followers of Christ, we had to give away everything we had, follow Christ only in poverty, and embrace the cross. When we opened the missal in the Church of San Nicola, we read: 'If you would be perfect, go, sell what you possess and give to the poor, and you will have treasure in heaven; and come, follow me'; 'Take nothing for your journey,' and 'If any man would come after me, let him deny himself and take up his cross daily and follow me.'"

Francis concluded, "And if you, too, wish to be 'perfect' followers of Christ, this is what Christ wants for you. This is what he wishes for each of you. These are the words of the Gospel! Be perfect! Choose penance! Live poorly! Pick up your cross and follow him!" With that, Francis genuflected toward the altar and withdrew.

Clare was spellbound. She stood there in the cathedral enraptured as the words of Francis struck her to the core. She had never heard anyone speak like him before. She had never heard such a sermon about the Incarnation and poverty in that way.

That night, Clare could not sleep as she lay in her bed. She could not stop thinking about Francis. There was something new and inspiring about him. His and the brothers' lives and actions corresponded perfectly to her thoughts about religion and faith. The way he was filled with the Spirit was like a magnet, and she felt drawn to him. Francis lived the Christian way of life that had been calling to her.

Clare got out of bed and went into the chapel where she placed herself before the crucifix. As she considered the words of Francis, she thought seriously about following him. She, too, wanted to live like him and the brothers. She, too, desired to love God and others charitably and to live in community with others doing the same—like Francis and the brothers.

And as she did, that flame that had always burned inside her began to grow more and more. She wanted to fully embrace poverty and experience the joy that accompanied it. Now she knew exactly what she wanted and how she wanted it: to be poor. Like Christ, like Mary. And now, like Francis. She wanted to become the first Franciscan woman.

> *Hearing of the then celebrated name of Francis, who, like a new man, was renewing with new virtues the way of perfection forgotten by the world, she was moved by the Father of the spirits—Whose initiatives each one had already accepted although in different ways—and immediately desired to see and hear him.*
>
> LEGEND 3:5

4

THE ENCOUNTER

My beloved speaks and says to me: "Arise, my love, my fair one, and come away."

SONG OF SOLOMON 2:10

YES, Clare was inspired. Deeply inspired. And she wanted to know him. She had to meet Francis and speak with him.[43] Francis, for his part, had also heard of Clare. He knew that she was a young noble woman from a Major family in upper Assisi. Yet he also knew that she was a woman of deep and devout prayer, that she loved the poor, and that she shunned her noble station in life. In all this, he knew that she was holy. Perhaps she was the woman of the prophecy, the woman who would follow him in San Damiano. Francis wanted to meet Clare, too.[44]

But such a meeting would have to be carefully orchestrated. Her father and uncles would never permit it. Therefore, they could know nothing about it. Clare expressed what was in her heart to Bona, Pacifica's sister. They were neighbors and Bona was trustworthy and pious. With the aid of Brother Rufino, Clare's cousin, Bona arranged a meeting with Francis at the cathedral. And there, in the presence of Assisi's patron, St. Rufino, Clare and Francis came face to face for the first time.

It was now the year 1211. Francis was a twenty-nine-year-old man while Clare, though mature, was still just seventeen years old. It is not an understatement to say that she had lived a sheltered life. Francis was twelve years her senior and was known through all the land by now. He had had a personal audience with Pope Innocent III, and he knew bishops and cardinals personally. As such, she felt apprehensive in his presence. Nonetheless, she trusted in her calling and was confident the Spirit had brought them together. She believed something important was about to happen.

Francis, for his part, felt the movement of the Holy Spirit strongly. He was there to encourage her. He spoke first.

"While I was praying for you today, Clare, the Lord revealed to me a message. When our Lord was in Bethany—the city of Mary, Martha, and Lazarus—he was reclining at the table of Simon, the leper."

Clare interjected, "And Mary came up to him with an alabaster jar of costly aromatic nard. And she poured it over his head."

Francis was impressed. "You are familiar with this Scripture, Clare?" he asked.

"Yes."

"What happened next?" asked Francis.

"She anointed the feet of Jesus, and dried his feet with her hair."

"And what did the disciples do?" he queried.

"The disciples became indignant. They admonished her saying, 'Why are you wasting this precious oil? It could have been sold for a lot of money, which we could have given to the poor.'"

"Did Jesus agree with their reasoning?" Francis asked.

"No. He admonished them for their logic. He said that she had done a good thing for him and asked the disciples why they made trouble for her. He then said, 'The poor you will always have with you, but you will not always have me.'"

"Why am I asking you this, Clare?" asked Francis.

Clare understood the meaning underlying the Scripture Francis was using to help her in her discernment.

She became visibly moved as she answered him, "Because Mary wasted her precious oil on Jesus," Clare said.

"In the eyes of the world, it was a waste for Mary to pour out the precious oil on Jesus." As Clare spoke, she thought of her father and uncles. "According to their worldly logic, the oil could have been sold, and the money earned, given to the poor. That would have been productive, practical, and good." Francis nodded.

She continued, "Yet Jesus admonished them for their worldly reasoning. He knew he would be with them only for a short time, while the poor would be with them always. He said that the precious oil would not be wasted on him."

"And why was it not a waste?" asked Francis.

Clare now began weeping as she said, "Because he loved Mary and wanted her sacrifice. He wanted everything she had." Clare knew what Francis was about to say to her next.

"Clare," responded Francis, "you are precious oil. Jesus loves you and he wants you to give yourself entirely to him. Give everything to him. Hold nothing back. Waste yourself on Jesus. He is worth it, and you will not be disappointed." At this, Bona and Rufino, too, were also moved, and their eyes sparkled with emotion.

Then Francis added, "But I must caution you. You will have to be prepared. In the eyes of the world, your sacrifice will make no sense. Many will admonish you for it, and they will not understand. They will reason according to the logic of the world. They will not see how a life spent hidden behind religious walls in prayer and virtue has any value. 'Sell the oil, and give the money to the poor!' They will cry as they try to convince you to marry a nobleman. But Jesus has another answer for you. And you know what it is. He will be your Most Noble Spouse. Clare, follow the desires your true Spouse has placed in your heart."

Francis and the others remained in silence for a moment as Clare closed her eyes and sat rapt in prayer with tears streaming down her face.

Finally, Francis posed one last question to her. "Clare, who was the disciple who was most adamant that Mary not give her oil to Jesus?"

"Judas," she said.

"You are correct, Clare. Do not let Judas make your decision for you. Judas will come for you, but do not be afraid. You are truly a light, Clare. And you shall shine for many. Trust in the Lord, Clare. Trust in the Lord."

Clare closed her eyes and said, "My mother planted the seed; you have watered me; but God will make me grow. I will be as your 'little plant.' Wherever you plant me, I will grow."[45] With that, Clare and Bona rose, bid farewell to the friars, and returned home.

Francis walked back to St. Mary of the Angels down in the valley with Brother Rufino. He felt consoled by the Lord. He knew that Clare was the woman he had been searching for. He believed that she was the fulfillment of the prophecy. *Indeed, it is not good for man to be alone*, he thought to himself.

A few years earlier, while he had dreamed of becoming a knight, she could have been his lady—his damsel. She was truly beautiful, charming, and faithful. She was full of life, spirit, purity, and innocence.

Women in the knightly tradition of courtly *Amor* of that era were often considered little more than objects of sensuality. Yearned after by knights in the courts of love, women were considered the highest "trophies"—rewards to the most competitive lover. Noblemen fought for the hearts of the women who were considered the most esteemed, courteous, courageous, skillful, gentle, ardent, gracious, beautiful, and honorable. And Clare was all these things.

But Francis was now serving a different Lord. And grace had transformed his carnal longings into spiritual ones. He no longer had the same desires. Yes, he desired Clare . . . but as a sister, nothing more. He was still a knight and she a lady. But now they were fighting battles of a different sort—spiritual ones, not earthly.

Clare, for her part, also viewed Francis as a courteous cavalier. He was chivalrous and gallant, brave and courageous. However, she would only have one love: Jesus Christ. Francis would never be her lover. Instead, he was as a troubadour to her: he was the one who passed through singing songs of love and the Lord. And the object of his love was the same object of hers. Together, they had one and the same true Love, the same true Lord. There was nothing more between them.

Francis and Clare loved one another as siblings. They were like twin souls—something akin to Scholastica and

Benedict of centuries earlier. Or they were like the future Jane Frances de Chantal and Francis de Sales. Together they would complement and support one another.

Clare would be like Mary, the one who listened quietly and intimately; Francis, instead, would be Martha, the one who served Christ's needs externally. Together, anima and animus, they would join hands spiritually and rebuild the Church together.

While their love for one another would grow, it would remain mutual and never exclusive. Their gaze would never be directed at one other; instead, they would look forward in the same direction at the same Person with the same desire. Their goal—the object of their gaze—was Jesus Christ. He was their Lord—the poor, minor crucified man on the cross.

Francis and Clare would be family to one another and to others. Francis would be like a father and brother to the sisters; Clare, in turn, would be a mother and sister to Francis and the brothers. They would become two giant trees who would shelter countless men and women in their shade.

Clare, accompanied always by Bona, continued meeting Francis secretly in the cathedral for about a year's time. He spoke to her about conversion and poverty. Clare listened to him intently and desired to do everything he told her.[46]

As she dialogued with Francis, joy and desire grew in her heart. She wanted to give up everything, embrace poverty, and follow Christ. She knew in her heart that giving away everything was not to embrace nothingness; instead, it was to empty herself of everything in order to allow God to fill it with himself. And as she grew in her vocation, he was already indeed filling her with joy, a joy she had never before experienced.

But though she wanted to follow him with all her heart, there were obstacles, enormous obstacles. Her father and uncles would never accept her decision. There was no way they would consent to her following Francis. They could never allow a daughter or niece of their status to join a rag-tag cluster of mendicants dedicated to poverty and minority. They had other plans for her. No, it seemed impossible, the hurdle insurmountable.

At times her doubts led to a sense of tremendous sorrow. The truth is that Clare loved her father deeply. When she gazed up at him, she saw a strong and powerful man. He was a knight, a descendant of the line of the first Holy Roman emperor, Charles the Great. She knew that he would do everything in his power to defend and protect her. She knew in her heart that he would sacrifice himself for her, giving even his own life. And she dreaded breaking his heart.

And what of her mother? It was her mother who had devoted herself totally to her. Ortulana had indeed planted the seed which had blossomed into a beautiful and fertile garden. Clare had never been away from her. And what of her sisters, especially Catherine? Clare was so close to Catherine, and she loved Beatrice dearly as well. How would she fare without her mother or her sisters?

Clare knew she did not have to say yes. She had the choice to marry the man, instead, chosen for her by others. Yes, even within the married state, she would be able to continue serving the poor, praying, and being generous with her possessions. She could one day teach her own children how to love God. And people would surely hear of her kindness and her light would shine. And all this would be good.

Yet she knew within her heart that if she chose not to follow Francis, the flame that was burning so intensely and brightly within her soul at that moment would be reduced forever to a mere flicker. Perhaps, at times, it would grow into a torch. But it would never be the blazing bonfire it was then at that moment.

For when Clare thought about giving up everything and living in true poverty, obedience, and chastity, she felt something within she had never before experienced. She knew it would be a sacrifice to live without worldly comforts and affections, but the thought of taking the veil left her feeling calm and serene. She would be "in the world" but not "of it." The thought strengthened her and gave her peace.

Clare was now keenly aware that she was no longer a child. She was a woman. Like Paul, Clare could now say to herself, "When I was a child, I spoke like a child, I thought like a child, I reasoned like a child; when I became [of age], I gave up childish ways" (1 Cor 13:11). She was now developing faithfulness to a different Father and was giving him her fidelity and obedience.

Clare thought of Francis and what he endured when he left his earthly father to embrace poverty. She was well acquainted with the story of how he left his worldly father to follow his eternal Father. She knew how Francis stripped himself of his last worldly vestments before his father, the bishop, and all the town. And he did so in order to break the bond that tied him and his earthly father, because he now had a new Father: "Our Father who art in heaven."

Clare wondered how her father would react. Would he be like Pharaoh? Would he seek to enslave her in his home as Pharaoh did the Jews in Egypt? Then how would she escape her "slavery" to the world? How would she be freed from the hands of her powerful Pharaoh? If she did leave and cross her Red Sea, would he follow her with his army and seek to bring her back? And then would God come and deliver her with a victory at the sea?

Or, Clare hoped, perhaps her earthly father would be more like Terah, the father of Abram. Her earthly father just might begin the journey with her as Terah accompanied his son, Abram, out of Ur of the Chaldeans on toward the land of Canaan. Would he walk toward her Promised Land with her?

Clare was torn as she thought about all these things. Clare knew what she had to do. But she did not know how to do it.

"I want to walk in the footsteps of Our Lord as you do, Francis. But how? I do not understand," Clare confided to Francis during one of their meetings together.

"To your question, Clare, I will respond with the words Christ gave to the rich young man who asked him what he needed to do to inherit eternal life. Christ first told him to obey the commandments. However, the man responded that he had always been obedient, as you have, too. So then Christ added that if he wished to be perfect, there was one thing left to do."

"Go, sell what you have, give the money to the poor, and come and follow me," Clare responded.

"You are right, Clare. But listen very closely to what I am about to tell you because here is the difference between being a 'good' follower of Christ and becoming his 'perfect' disciple. Jesus wants you to do more than merely give of your belongings to the poor, though this is good. Instead, he wants you to give everything. And in giving away everything, you will become something you are not." Clare listened very closely to what Francis was saying.

He continued, "Just as the Second Person of the Trinity became something he was not—incarnate and human—when the Word 'emptied himself, taking the form of a servant, being born in the likeness of men,' you, too, must empty yourself and become something you are not." Clare nodded.

"When I was in the world, before I began doing penance, I sought to become greater in the world—a nobleman, a great knight," Francis continued. "I sought to become *Major*, or someone of your father's class. In effect, I was seeking to become something I was not, something *greater*. However, after I discovered the true Christ and began doing penance, I sought to do what he did and become like him. I sought to become *lesser*. Thus, I renounced my worldly wealth and my status and class as a Minor and sought to become a true minor, like Christ." Clare then began to understand what Christ meant by being a "perfect follower."

"Clare, to follow Christ perfectly, you must renounce your status and become something you are not. You must become lesser than what you are. It is not enough to just *give* to the poor. Instead, you must *become* poor. You must embrace *all* the poverty of the Christ who humbled himself as he became man and walked in this world and suffered his passion and went to the cross. In doing this, you will become the perfect disciple of Christ and you will become a true minor. For you will become like him."

Clare's heart was full of joy as she understood now what it would mean to follow Christ the way Francis did.

"But unlike the rich young man who went away full of sadness, I will rejoice," she added.

"And in doing so, you will, indeed, find treasure in heaven," Francis rejoined.

"I am sure of it," she said. "But as a follower of Christ in poverty, where will I live? What will I eat? You are men and you work for alms or go into the towns and beg for them," she said. "I, however, will not be able to do that. How will we be provided for?"

"Clare, do not worry about the things of this world and what you will eat and what you will wear, 'for if God so clothes the grass of the field, which today is alive and tomorrow is thrown into the oven, will he not much more clothe you?' The Lord loves you and will provide for you. You can trust him," he exhorted her.

"Clare, you must learn to live in this world as 'a stranger and exile on this earth.' What shall happen of you is a mystery to us now. But God will show us the way. You can trust him. He will never disappoint you," Francis assured her.

"God wills this," Francis added. "And his providence is working it out. We are making provisions to bring your departure to fruition. Remember that your peace is in his will. 'The LORD will fight for you, and you have only to be still.'"

Clare felt like she had hitherto been a merchant searching for fine pearls. But now she had truly found that great Pearl of great price. And she was about to go and sell all to buy it.

Throughout this period of trial and preparation, she kept her gaze fixed on one Person: Jesus Christ. And as she did, her heart pined, desire welled, joy abounded.

> *[Francis] visited her and she more frequently him, moderating the times of their visits so that this divine pursuit could not be perceived by anyone nor objected to by gossip. For, with only one close companion accompanying her, the young girl, leaving her paternal home, frequented the clandestine meetings with the man of God, whose words seemed to her to be on fire and whose deeds were seen to be beyond the human. The Father Francis encouraged her to despise the world, showing her by his living speech how dry the hope of the world was and how deceptive its beauty. He whispered in her ears of a sweet espousal with Christ, persuading her to preserve the pearl of her virginal purity for that blessed Spouse Whom Love made man.*
>
> LEGEND 3:5

5

FUGA MUNDI—FLIGHT FROM THE WORLD

You have ravished my heart, my sister, my bride, you have ravished my heart with a glance of your eyes, with one jewel of your necklace.

SONG OF SOLOMON 4:1

IT was Lent in the year 1212.[47] Clare was now eighteen years old; she was of age. The "fragrant flower" was ready. The "star of Assisi" was willing. The foundation had been prepared and many had taken part. The Lord had indeed provided.

Before her departure, she put her practical affairs in order. There was only one condition that Francis required of all his followers. If someone wanted to walk in the footsteps of Christ the way he did, they had to do just one thing. And it did not matter if that person was wealthy or poor, of noble birth or a commoner, educated or illiterate. A man, or now, a woman. If anyone wanted to follow Francis in the footsteps of Christ, he (now she) had to carry out just one scriptural verse. And they had to do it literally: "If you would be perfect, go, sell what you possess and give to the poor, and you will have treasure in heaven; and come, follow me" (Mt 19:21).

It complemented the other two scriptural verses that were revealed to Francis and which would become the ultimatum for all Franciscan followers. Francis opened the missal in the Church of San Nicola in the center of Assisi and read, "Take nothing for your journey" (Lk 9:3) and, "If any man would come after me, let him deny himself and take up his cross daily and follow me" (Lk 9:23).

These commands made up the one ironclad imperative for all Francis's followers: poverty. Though Francis was often flexible when it came to other religious rules and observances, he was rigid on this one. There were no exceptions. The fact that Clare was a woman made no difference. She, too, would have to sell or leave her possessions and inheritance, renounce her birthright and status, and follow Christ as a minor, a lesser.

And she did all this, as her own sister, Beatrice, later testified: "[Clare] sold her entire inheritance and part of that of [Beatrice's] and gave it to the poor." Now she was fully ready.[48]

The day of Clare's departure was carefully chosen as it was the feast commemorating Jesus's triumphal entry into Jerusalem days before his crucifixion: Palm Sunday.[49] On the final Sunday of Lent, marking the beginning of the great Holy Week, Jesus enters Jerusalem not riding a horse, a great steed of war, as was the expectation of the people for their hoped-for Messiah, the Christ, the Anointed One. Instead, he arrives on the back of a young donkey, symbolizing his presence among them as a man of humility and simplicity. The people welcome him with palms and olive branches—the symbol of peace and victory—as a sign of homage and great respect.

Thus, Palm Sunday would be the day Clare would leave her "world" behind and enter her "New Jerusalem." She, too, would renounce the "war-horse" of her noble status and splendor and embrace the "donkey" of her simplicity and poverty. The palms of Christ's victory could easily have been her "lily,"—the symbol of purity, flower of the Virgin.

Dressed in her finest garments, she would receive her prize: the palm branch. She had spent that Lent preparing spiritually for what may indeed be her own Friday passion. But she knew without a doubt that hers would also be a Sunday resurrection.

When it came time for Mass, Guido, the bishop of Assisi, was at the altar. He watched Clare as she arrived with her sisters and the women of her household and took her place in the rear of the church.[50] Clare was clothed beautifully in her finest gown and jewelry. While the other noblewomen and distinguished ladies took their privileged places in the front of the church near the altar, Clare remained in the rear. Bishop Guido, the same prelate who had overseen Francis's parting from his father some years earlier, would also play a role in Clare's separation from hers.

When the time came during the Mass for the blessing of the olive branches, which were used in place of palms in Assisi, Bishop Guido sprinkled holy water and incensed them. The people came up to the altar one by one to receive their gift. Clare, however, remained in the rear, motionless.

After Bishop Guido distributed the olive branches to the faithful, he watched her. Though he was known for being proud and hot-tempered, a moment of sensitivity overcame him. He stepped down from the altar, went to her, and personally placed the branch in her hand, acknowledging her with a paternal nod. Clare gazed up into his eyes and knew he was in agreement with her decision. He knew what she was about to undertake; indeed, he had helped arrange her departure. That night the eighteen-year-old girl would secretly escape her home with its worldly privileges to follow Francis with only one privilege: poverty.[51]

Clare's father and uncle noticed the curious exchange between Clare and the bishop from a distance. They looked at one another with concern, grave concern. Clare returned home and spent the remainder of the day praying intensely in the chapel.

After nightfall, Clare was ready. She had rehearsed the plan mentally numerous times. After the others went to sleep, she arose quietly from her bed and awoke her younger sister, Catherine. She knew what was about to happen and played her part. Catherine helped Clare put on the same dress and noble garments she had worn at Mass only a few hours earlier. She adorned Clare's hair—still beautifully braided—with a garland of flowers.

Clare looked at Catherine and kissed her on the cheek as they embraced. "Farewell, sister. Pray it all goes well. It won't be long," Clare told her. They had plans for Catherine's future as well, and their separation would, hopefully, be brief.

Clare walked alone down the stairs and then down the cold and drafty corridor by candlelight. She walked swiftly but soundlessly, so as not to wake anyone. The candle she was carrying cast eerie shadows on the walls behind the instruments of war and the family coat of arms.

As Clare began her journey, she was feeling anxious. However, she also believed in her heart that she was following the will of God. She inaudibly prayed over and over the prayers Francis had taught her. Soon she came to possess a supernatural strength not her own. Despite her fears, she kept moving.

She arrived at the end of the hallway and stopped at the minor door, sometimes called the "door of the dead." She avoided the main door, as the paid guardsman sat outside it with his crossbow keeping vigil over their house in addition to the cathedral and other noble houses in the district. It was fitting that she used the "door of the dead," as that night she was forever dying to herself and to her world. She blew the dust off the heavy wooden beam and the thick iron bar. With a strength not her own, she lifted the beam and the bar that barricaded it shut.[52]

She stepped outside the door and looked around for her companion who would help her make the journey that night. Up and to her right were the remnants of the old feudal castle still watching over Assisi. To her left was the Cathedral of San Rufino.

In a few moments, a woman stepped out of the darkness and whispered forcefully, "Clare!" It was Pacifica, Bona's sister. Pacifica was the same woman who had accompanied Clare's mother, Ortulana, when she had left Assisi on her own pilgrimage eighteen years earlier.[53]

Clare and Pacifica embraced and then scurried among the shadows of Assisi's cathedral walls. They avoided the openness of the square and the wide Via Parlascio as they were afraid someone might see them; women like them did not walk the streets of Assisi at night. They moved hurriedly among the alleyways and stayed close to the numerous palaces of the upper nobility as they descended the stone staircases.

As they went down to the central part of Assisi, they circumvented the exposed Piazza Grande (the large square) where the Minors lived. They passed by the shops of notaries, butchers, tax collectors, cobblers, bakers, masons, and barbers. Clare and Pacifica then went down another staircase in an alleyway. Clare glanced to her right: she was passing by the house of Francis's irascible father, Pietro of Bernardone, and his pious mother, Pica. Not far to her left was the small Church of San Giorgio by the city gate. There some priests ran a school where they had taught Francis basic Latin grammar as a boy. Clare had no way of knowing that in some fifty years, a massive Gothic basilica would be built next to that church to forever safeguard her body.

Assisi could be a magical place, especially in the dark. That early spring night was peculiarly quiet, and the soft moonlight and torchlight cast a warm and inviting hue over the city's cream-colored buildings constructed of stone carved out of Mount Subasio. Clare, however, took no notice of the city's nocturnal magnificence and the sights she was seeing very likely for the last time. She was oblivious to the houses with their facades and balconies, the churches and bell towers, the washing fountains and cisterns, the cobblestone streets. Instead, her heart and mind were fixed on her destination.

Finally, the pair passed behind the apse of the former cathedral of Assisi, Santa Maria Maggiore—still the residence of Assisi's bishop, Guido. They had almost arrived at the lowest part of the Assisi city walls near the city gate of

Moiano. Clare's heart raced as she and Pacifica approached the gate.

It had been negotiated for the guard to open the door for the two when they arrived. Clare looked anxiously over her shoulder as the sentinel unhurriedly removed the huge wooden beam and unfastened the thick creaky bolt. Finally, in what seemed an eternity, he pushed the giant city door open just enough for the two small women to pass through. Pacifica took out a coin from her purse and gave it to him as they passed by.

As the two walked away from Assisi, the loud thud startled Clare as the heavy beam fell back into place behind her in the darkness. She quickened her pace as she heard the squeaky metal dead bolt slide back into its thick hinges. She was walking so fast that Pacifica had a hard time keeping up with her. She dreaded hearing the sound of galloping horses behind her any minute now.

"Slow down, Clare, there's no one there!" Pacifica said, trying to console her.

As the two walked under the moonlight down the steep old road toward the valley, a sense of serenity soon calmed Clare's agitated state. The uneasiness subsided and peace began to return to her heart. It was at this point that Clare became fully cognizant of what had just happened: she had just "left the world."

Like the desert mothers and fathers of old who left their native cities to dwell in the desert—alone and with nothing—Clare, too, left the world of her youth with all her family, friends, and familiarity. In the most traditional sense of the term, what Clare was doing that night was a very real *fuga mundi*, a "flight from the world."

Clare's entire "world" was Assisi. The city—with her family and companions, its people and churches, its customs and ways—was all she knew. Prior to that night, she may have only rarely been outside those city walls. The walls, indeed, did more than defend the city from attack: they guarded within them a sense of community, citizenship, and ways of doing things. Those city walls delineated and defined the Assisian culture; inside those walls, things were done a certain way.

Clare, for her part, had to leave that world. Only by leaving it could she fully and truly embrace the new life she was called to. The Lord had revealed to her that her journey was to follow Francis in the footsteps of the poor, lesser, minor Christ. To stay in that world would have meant to remain within its societal structure of materialism and classism, which would have thwarted the Spirit that was growing within her. Thus, Clare had to flee from her world.

However, Clare could never have "hated the world"—though such language was commonly used in religious monasteries then. For Clare would remain forever connected to the world in her new life. Yet it would only be from outside the "world" where she could offer that same world an alternative. Thus, she had to flee.

And like the desert mothers and fathers, she did not know where she was going. She only knew what her first step was and where she was going that night. Afterwards, the rest would be revealed. She was in the hands of Providence.

As the pair passed the cluster of homes and towers known as Valecchie, they were about halfway to their first destination that night. When Clare and her companion reached the old road, the Via Antiqua, at the valley floor, they turned right.

Soon they arrived at the leper hospital, known locally as the Ospedaletto. Clare thought of Francis. In that very spot, he had once embraced a leper. Francis, too, had given up the wealth and security of his father's house in the well-to-do neighborhood of the Minors in central Assisi to live as a penitent near the lepers. That embrace marked the turning point in his conversion, as it was also an embrace of minority—lesserness.

Though Clare would never encounter a leper in such a way, she was nonetheless descending that night toward lesserness. She, too, was "emptying herself" of the wealth and nobility of her father's house in upper Assisi and was descending to the depths of the valley floor. There, where the lepers and thieves dwelt, she, too, was dying to herself.

And in this, she was following not only her earthly teacher, Francis but also their heavenly teacher, Jesus Christ. For it was the Second Person of the Trinity, the Word, who humbled himself the most by descending from "heaven's royal throne" and taking on human flesh in the womb of a virgin. He then humbled himself further by accepting death on the cross with criminals. Yet the Lord of lords went further: he descended to the dead.

Clare pondered these things in her heart as the two women turned left and walked along the old road known as the Via della Portiuncula that traversed the valley from Assisi to the villages of Costano and then to Bettona.

Soon, from within the dense forest ahead of her, she began to see a warm glow of lights moving toward her. Tears streamed down her face when she realized it was

Francis and the brothers carrying torches! The men were moved, too, to finally have a sister, whom they embraced warmly. Under a clear moonlit sky, the men returned with their first female companion back to the Church of St. Mary of the Angels where they lived.

Because it was dedicated to St. Mary, the Queen of the Angels, this was Francis's favorite place in the world. It was known locally as the Portiuncula since it was located on a small "portion of land." Owned by the Benedictines of Mt. Subasio, Francis and the brothers still gave the monks a basket of fish each year as a type of rent to stay there. But Francis also loved it because it was there that he was moved to fully embrace poverty.[54] St. Mary of the Angels was one of the three churches Francis rebuilt with his own hands.[55]

But that night, another event that would pass into Franciscan legend would take place at the little country church: it would be the site of Clare's celestial wedding marking her entrance into religion and the Franciscan way of life.

Standing before the altar dedicated to the Virgin Mary, Clare removed her smooth outer gown, her beautiful and noble dress in the world. In its stead, Francis gave her the rough penitential habit, her celestial bridal dress—beautiful and noble in the spirit. Clare slipped into the grayish-white tunic made of undyed wool. She then tied it with the rope cord. No possession, tool, or money bag would ever hang from it: she would remain poor for life.

Clare then kneeled while Francis removed her worldly jewels and garland from her head. Then, with the same crude shears used to shave sheep, Francis "razed" her head personally, giving her the tonsure.[56] The long flowing hair of the lovely young virgin—the object and symbol of desire, youth, and beauty—was severed. The tresses of the young noblewoman of Assisi—which hitherto had been adorned with diadems, wreaths, flowers, and headbands and braided with golden or silk threads—now lay in clumps on the cold stone floor. Clare would never delight an earthly husband with that hair. She would now seek to please, instead, her heavenly Spouse.

Finally, Francis covered Clare's shaved head with a veil. The tonsure and veil would be the sign of Clare's decision to give herself to God and him alone. She was now fully and wholly consecrated to God, her celestial and most noble Spouse. She was a virgin only for Christ.[57]

Clare remained on her knees before the altar in blissful ecstasy as she contemplated her new life and her new Spouse. Now in spirit, she could truly say to herself, "I will greatly rejoice in the Lord, my soul shall exult in my God; for he has clothed me with the garments of salvation, he has covered me with the robe of righteousness, as a bridegroom decks himself with a garland, and as a bride adorns herself with her jewels" (Is 61:10).

However, her flight that night was not yet complete. She could not stay long.

"Francis, we have to go," said Rufino. "Now . . . We can't stay here. She's not safe . . ."

Therefore, when [Palm] Sunday came, the young girl, thoroughly radiant with festive splendor among the crowd of women, entered the Church with the others. Then something occurred that was a fitting omen: as the others were going [to receive] the palms, while Clare remained immobile in her place out of shyness, the Bishop, coming down the steps, came to her and placed a palm in her hands. On that night, preparing to obey the command of the saint, she embarked upon her long desired flight with a virtuous companion. . . . And so she ran to Saint Mary of the Portiuncula, leaving behind her home, city, and relatives. There the brothers, who were observing sacred vigils before the little altar of God, received the virgin Clare with torches. There, immediately after rejecting the filth of Babylon, she gave the world a 'bill of divorce.' There, her hair shorn by the hands of the brothers, she put aside every kind of fine dress. Was it not fitting that an Order of flowering virginity be awakened in the evening or in any other place than in this place of her the first and most worthy of all, who alone is Mother and Virgin!

LEGEND 4:7–8

6

SAN PAOLO OF THE ABBESSES

How sweet is your love, my sister, my bride! how much better is your love than wine, and the fragrance of your oils than any spice!

SONG OF SOLOMON 4:10

WITHOUT delay, Francis and some of the friars left the Portiuncula with Clare and Pacifica. They could not afford to dally, as Clare's relatives could come at any moment. They walked determinedly in the valley to the north by torchlight. With Assisi in view to their right, Clare became apprehensive again as she thought she heard horses galloping in the distance.

The band of poor penitents crossed the little wooden bridge over the Tescio River. Their feet got wet, as the river was full of gushing water from the melting snows coming off Mount Subasio. They cautiously avoided the road, known as the Campiglione, that ran from Assisi to the villages of Petrignano and Isola Romana (now Bastia). Instead, they took the little trail along the banks of the river under the cover of the forest.

Finally, just before the Tescio fed into the larger Chiascio River (which in turn flowed into the mighty Tiber a short distance later on its way south to Rome), they arrived.

Clare breathed a sigh of relief when she saw her destination for the night—and for the foreseeable future. She knew she was safe now.

It was a few hours before dawn. Francis banged lightly on the heavy metal knocker. Someone promptly slid open the small face-sized panel in the upper part of the door. A woman's voice spoke gently through the grate asking who was there.

"It's us—Francis and Clare," said Francis. The metal bolts immediately slid open and the thick wooden door opened up.

Francis and Clare looked at one another and embraced. They did not have to speak, as each knew what was in the other's heart. Clare then stepped inside the door, which closed behind her. The friars took the Campiglione Road to accompany Pacifica back to Assisi.

It was finished now. The "conversion" of Clare of Assisi was complete. She had fully left the world and was now standing inside a Benedictine monastery for women. However, though by all appearances it seemed as if Clare had entered religion according to conventional norms and traditions established centuries earlier, Clare's approach to religion would soon prove unique.

The formal name of the women's monastery was St. Paul of the Handmaidens (San Paolo delle Ancelle), though it was known by the locals more colloquially as St. Paul of the Abbesses (San Paolo delle Abbadesse). The nuns of San Paolo followed the Rule of St. Benedict, and their monastery was the most prominent for women in the territory of Assisi. Renowned throughout the land for its wealth and influence, its properties included vast tracts of land on both sides of the Chiascio River, estates near Isola Romana, cottages and gardens near the churches of San Pietro, Sant'Andrea, and Santo Stefano in Assisi, groves of olives, vineyards, and more. Numerous serfs and farmers worked the holdings for the nuns, providing them with cash payments and rents while armed guards patrolled the territory.

Due to its prominence, San Paolo was also known for the noblewomen from the most illustrious Assisi families who entered there. When they made vows, they further enriched the monastery with large dowries and gifts from wealthy relatives and benefactors. Noblewomen in monasteries were known as *choristae* (choir nuns), and they spent their lives primarily praying the Liturgy of the Hours and studying Scripture in what is called *lectio divina.*

On the other hand, there were also the *conversae* (lay sisters) who lived on the monastic grounds. The *conversae* lived separate lives from the *choristae*: they slept, prayed, worked, and ate in entirely distinct quarters. Many of the lay sisters there had been servants or ladies-in-waiting to the noblewomen before their lady entered the monastery. And when the noblewomen took the veil, the servants followed them, where they continued to live as servants.

Other lay sisters were country girls from the families of poor commoners when they felt the call to enter the monastery. Being illiterate and uneducated, they were ignorant of Latin and thus could not pray the Psalter and participate in the canonical Hours. Their station in life, plus the fact that they did not have dowries, necessitated that they play ancillary roles in the monastery, such as doing menial work in the kitchen or in the fields. Their manual labor kept the monastery functioning and provided the choir nuns with more time to pray and study. Some of them also served as extern sisters of the community—those whose role it was to greet visitors and handle relations between the cloistered nuns and the outside world.

The portress who had just opened the door for Clare greeted her with a warm welcome and an embrace. "I've been waiting for you all night," she said excitedly. "Mother Abbess and Donna Prioress told me you were coming this night, but she did not say when. I am sorry for your circumstances, but I hope your journey went well."[58]

"It did, Sister, thank you," responded Clare. She couldn't help noticing that the lay sister's accent and way of speaking revealed she was from Assisi's commoner class. "Thank you for taking me in, especially at this hour," she added.

"Of course. We are happy to have you here. Come, Donna Clare, let me show you to your sleeping quarters. You must be exhausted. My name is Sister Angela."[59]

"Thank you, Sister Angela," replied the new penitent as she followed the extern sister down the long corridor. It was lined with icons of saints and other holy images. "And please call me Sister," Clare added. [60]

"All right, if that is your wish," responded Sister Angela with a strange look on her face. She thought that was an odd request for a woman of Clare's status to make.

"I've already had your bed prepared in one of the comfortable apartments in the quarters of the *choristae*," Sister Angela said as she continued leading Clare down the long corridor.

Clare winced but quickly hid her disapproval. When they reached the end of the corridor, there was more light. There the sister got her first good look at Clare. She stood there in shock as she eyed Clare up and down, dismayed at her appearance.

Clare spoke up. "Sister, it is my desire to stay not with the *choristae*, but instead with the *conversae*."

"Oh my," replied the sister, distressed at Clare's rough undyed tunic and bare feet in addition to her abnormal request.

"Donna Clare . . . I mean *Sister* Clare," responded Sister Angela. "I think I must have made a mistake. I thought Donna Prioress said you were the daughter of a Major of Assisi, a knight. Did I misunderstand her? You are *Lady Clare*, the daughter of Sir Favarone of Offreduccio, are you not?"

"Yes, Sister Angela, it is I, Clare, the daughter of Favarone of Offreduccio and Ortulana, the daughter of Fiumi. However, I do not wish to stay with the *choristae*. Instead, it is my desire to stay in the quarters with the *conversae*."

"You want to stay with us?" Sister Angela shot back, bewildered. "I do not think Donna Prioress would approve . . ." she stammered in amazement. "I . . . I . . . I would have to wake her and get her permission. I am not sure what to do . . ."

"It is all right, Sister Angela," Clare interjected seeking to reassure the apprehensive sister. "I will stay with the *choristae* this night. Tomorrow I will speak with your superiors, Mother Abbess or Donna Prioress, and express my wish directly to either of them."

"All right . . ." replied Sister Angela as she opened the door to Clare's apartment, now concerned that the mental faculties of the monastery's guest were not quite right.

She then said to Clare, "Donna Clare . . . I mean, *Sister* Clare, Donna Prioress told me to let you know that the choir nuns will be praying morning Lauds at dawn, which will be soon. You will hear the bells. If you wish, you may join them." Clare thanked her for the invitation.

"But I must tell you something . . ." Sister Angela continued nervously. "I am sure she and the abbess will not approve if you arrive dressed as you are now, especially as this is Holy Week. There are prayer cloaks at the entrance to the choir, which I suppose you could use to cover yourself."

"Thank you and good night," replied Clare politely.

"And good night to you, *Sister* Clare," replied the extern sister. As she disappeared down the corridor, she had a peculiar sensation that something out of the ordinary was about to happen there in the good monastery of San Paolo.

Clare entered her room and looked around. Its furnishings consisted of a decorative oak chest, a gilded trestle table and chair, a high bed surrounded by curtains, a fireplace, and wall tapestries. It was not very different from the luxurious room she had just left in her father's home only a few hours earlier. Instead of lying down on the comfortable mattress, however, she kneeled down before the cross on the wall and spent what remained of the night in prayer.

The extern sister, instead of returning to her cell, however, went straight to the prioress's apartment and waited outside her door for her to arise. When dawn came and the bells rang, the prioress came out of her apartment. Sister Angela immediately recounted everything while the prioress listened attentively. The prioress then went straight to the abbess and told her, in turn, everything she had just learned about their new guest. She, too, listened gravely with concern.

The abbess presided solemnly over morning Lauds. The *choristae* nuns wore veils on their heads and wimples around their faces. Their black habits and scapulars were covered by the prayer shawl. They stood, sat, or kneeled in beautifully handcrafted wooden choir stalls. All the while, the abbess's jewel-encrusted crozier—the staff or rook denoting the rank of bishop, abbot, or abbess—stood commandingly at her side. As it was Holy Week, the liturgy was particularly poignant and the psalms were chanted majestically and flawlessly in Latin. The abbess and prioress glanced frequently at the entrance to the choir waiting for their guest to arrive. She never did.

Meanwhile, just after dawn, Pacifica returned to Assisi. Francis and the friars accompanied her to the city gate near the men's monastery of San Pietro, where they saluted her and continued back to St. Mary of the Angels. When Pacifica arrived near her home on the San Rufino square across from Favarone's castle, she noticed frenzied activity taking place across the square and became alarmed. She pulled up her hood covering her head and quickened her pace.

Though she had anticipated as much, she was startled by how many knights and guards on horseback were coming and going. Pacifica entered into her home and bolted the door behind her. She took a deep breath and said quietly to herself, *Deo gratias!* (Thanks be to God). It was finished. While many may never see Clare again, Pacifica knew that she would, very soon.

Clare, meanwhile, had found her way to the quarters of the lay sisters, where she joined them in their own morning prayers. They dressed in religious tunics different from those of the *choristae*. Theirs were of lighter material and were brownish-gray, instead of black. The prayers of the lay sisters were brief, consisting mostly of devotions to Mary, the angels, and saints in addition to rote prayers like *Paters*, *Aves*, and *Glorias*, which they said on beads.[61]

In the spirit of Franciscan poverty, Clare knew she could not stay with the choir nuns. She had not just surrendered the privileges of her father's house for the privileges of a monastic house. She did not renounce the wealth and security of her worldly home for the wealth and security of a religious home. She was now a follower of Francis in the footsteps of the lesser, poor Christ. Thus, she had to refuse the monastic privileges of the *choristae* that were indeed hers through birthright and custom. She had to give up her inheritance and noble status and arrive in religion not as a noblewoman but as a servant!

Clare planned on spending her time there in San Paolo with the *conversae*.[62] However, it might not be as simple as she hoped. Indeed, while Clare was orienting herself on the grounds of the *conversae*, Sister Angela came running up to her, "Clare, come with me. Mother Abbess wishes to speak with you . . . Immediately!"

Clare obediently followed the portress, who led her hastily to the other side of the monastic grounds. When they arrived at the quarters of the *choristae*, Sister Angela led Clare to the abbess's study. She told Clare to wait outside while she entered.

Sister Angela entered the study, knelt obediently, bowed her head, and said, "Most Reverend Mother Abbess, I am here with Donna Clare."

"Send her in," responded the abbess solemnly without looking up from a ledger. Sister Angela dutifully exited the study and returned with Clare who likewise went humbly to her knees before the abbess.

As Clare knelt before her, the abbess took a few moments to finish her work. Clare was struck by her appearance. Though small in size, her demeanor was imposing and authoritative. She was seated on an ornately decorated cathedra-like throne with her crozier at her side. Her face was framed within a wimple while a long, majestic veil descended behind her below her waist. She wore a black woolen habit that was tied with a heavy leather belt around her waist. Over her habit was a knee-length rectangular scapular. She wore white gloves with decorative lace protruding from under the sleeves. As abbess, she wore an ornate gold chain around her neck with a large gold cross adorned with precious stones. Her prioress was dressed similarly to the abbess, absent the pectoral cross. She stood at her abbess's side.

The abbess's name was Sibilia.[63]

After wrapping up her ledger and handing it to her prioress, Abbess Sibilia looked up for the first time. She asked Clare politely how the night had gone. Her courteous way of speaking revealed she was from the upper nobility.

"Very well, thank you, Mother Abbess," replied Clare respectfully before the two rulers of the honorable monastery of San Paolo of the Abbesses.

"You may stand," replied the abbess. It was at that moment when she and the prioress got their first full look at Clare. The prioress raised her eyebrows in surprise while the abbess stared at her up and down for what seemed to Clare a long time.

Finally, the abbess broke the silence. "The august and most venerable bishop of Assisi, Lord Guido, has communicated to me everything, Donna Clare. I am aware of your situation," she said.

"Thank you, Most Reverend Abbess, for accepting . . ."

"However," she cut Clare off, "I was not informed that you, Donna Clare, a noblewoman, daughter of the esteemed house of Favarone, had overnight been transformed into a pauper," she said severely. As she said this, she and the prioress exchanged glances expressing their mutual disapproval.

After a pause, the mature Sibilia continued her discourse to the young penitent before her. "Donna Clare, your station and background, your status as a noblewoman and daughter of a Major of Assisi—a knight and lord no less—necessitate that you live in religion according to certain norms. You are not a servant. It is neither decorous nor fitting for you to dress in that manner. Nor is it appropriate that you continue to associate with the *conversae*," she said sternly.

"Reverend Mother, I know and understand the religious customs," Clare replied good-naturedly. "However, as a follower of the poor, lesser Christ, I wish to follow him in the footsteps of Francis and live as Christ did, as a poor minor."

At the mention of Francis's name, Sibilia sighed loudly. "I know of the ways of Francis," she retorted. "He is a pious Christian who loves the Lord and religion . . . notwithstanding, however, his eccentricities. He speaks of poverty and even insinuates that Our Lord is poor. However, is not Christ the Second Person of the Most Holy Trinity? Is he not Our Lord through whom all things were made?" The abbess paused as if awaiting a response, though her questions were rhetorical. Clare remained silent. The abbess continued.

"Is Christ not the Son of God the Father, the transcendent Creator of the heavens and earth? Is our God not the God for whom every knee shall bow, every tongue shall swear? He is, indeed! As such, religion necessitates decorum . . . Our religious life demands it!" She paused again.

"God is almighty in heaven and earth because he is the Creator of heaven and earth whose order he established and which remains subject to him at his disposal. God existed before the world and is, thus, outside of the world. God has revealed himself as holy, mysterious, incomprehensible, and omnipotent. God is transcendent." The abbess paused again, this time for dramatic effect.

"The way we present ourselves, therefore, in religion," she continued, "especially at worship—our comportment, our manner—is of utmost significance. We must strive to mirror the glory of God. And this is particularly true regarding our custom of dress." As she said this, she gestured her hand toward her habit and then toward Clare's tunic, contrasting the differences.

Clare remained silent, though she was thinking how distant the abbess's words made God seem to her. Though Clare would never have disputed the transcendent nature of God, she thought to herself how often Francis emphasized how the same God drew close to humanity.

Francis, too, often used Scripture to describe the Lord when he preached: "See how He humbles Himself (see Phil 2:8) as when He came from heaven's royal throne (see Wis

18:15) into the womb of the Virgin; daily He comes to us in a humble form; daily He comes down from the bosom of the Father upon the altar in the hands of the priest. And as He appeared to the holy apostles in true flesh, so now He reveals Himself to us in the sacred bread."[64] However, this was neither the time nor the place to debate. Clare would let her actions be her words.

"God is truth and law," Abbess Sibilia pronounced authoritatively. "Therefore, religion requires proper and just authority in its administration. Order and *stablitas* first and foremost! Our Lord demands dignity, propriety, and respectability. Not living in pigsties as Francis and his brothers do. Nonetheless, Bishop Guido is someway fond of Francis and his little community . . . And apparently also of *you*. In fact, I have agreed to offer you hospitality here only at his behest.

"However," she continued, "the friars are men, and they are strong. You are a woman. A *noble* woman. You are not accustomed to his ways of 'poverty.' It will prove too difficult for you. You will see. I am sure of it." To the abbess, Clare was inexperienced and, quite frankly, naive.

"Thank you for your admonitions, Reverend Mother Abbess. However, I must insist on staying with the *conversae*. Please, I beg you," implored Clare.

The abbess was struck by Clare's willingness to challenge her. "Donna Clare, you are indeed bold and most tenacious. This is a trait you have surely acquired from the knights of your family. I must say that I expected your presence here to cause troubles arising from *outside* this monastery due to your family's opposition to your entrance into religion. I did not expect difficulties to come from *within . . .*" Abbess Sibilia paused for a moment as she considered her options.

"Though I am contrary to your proposition—and such an entreaty has never been made here . . . *ever*—I will, nevertheless, not deny you your request. If such is your will, though errant and misguided as I believe it to be, I give my consent. However, I must first confer with Bishop Guido to ensure there are no religious proscriptions against it. If there are not, then you have my permission to stay with the servants. In time, you will come to see the folly of your ways."

"Thank you, Mother Abbess," replied Clare joyfully.

"Donna Prioress, please have the extern sister accompany Donna Clare to her new quarters . . . with the *conversae* . . . And have one of them prepare a cell for her. She may stay with them and pray with them. She may also join them in their day's work . . . *their most laborious day's work*. Good day, Donna Clare."

Clare bowed reverently to the abbess and turned to leave.

"Donna Clare," the abbess said stopping her. Clare turned around. "There is one more thing . . . As of now, few people know you are here. But soon, many will know. Spend this Holy Week preparing yourself accordingly." Abbess Sibilia then promptly returned her attention back to the stack of ledgers before her.

The prioress dutifully escorted Clare out of the study and passed along the abbess's instructions to Sister Angela who was waiting outside. She then accompanied Clare back to the quarters of the *conversae*. There Clare was overjoyed at overcoming her first obstacle in San Paolo, even if she knew that the major one was yet to come.

Clare spent Holy Week praying with the *conversae* sisters and working with them in the kitchen and in the garden. She did whatever was needed and required. The lay sisters were delighted that an actual noble lady was living among them, even if initially they were confused by her presence.

"Donna Clare, why are you here?" a simple lay sister asked Clare one morning while stitching the habit of one of the choir nuns. Her strong country accent revealed she was from a peasant family.

"Sister, it is true that I come from the nobility. But what does Christ want from us?" asked Clare. "Father Francis, my teacher and guide, taught me many things. He taught me humility in the words of Christ, who said, 'The last will be first, and the first last'; 'He who is greatest among you shall be your servant; whoever exalts himself will be humbled, and whoever humbles himself will be exalted.' Some of the sisters paused from their work and listened to Clare as she spoke.

"He taught me to love poverty with the words of Christ, who said, 'Blessed are the poor in spirit, for theirs is the kingdom of heaven.' But here the Lord does not love the poverty that leads to misery and grief, as Our Lord does not bless the poverty of suffering," she continued. "Instead, he wants us, like him, to embrace humility and simplicity. This is the Lord we follow and this is the poverty we wish to practice." By now all the lay sisters had stopped working and had gathered around Clare.

"As a follower of the footsteps of Christ," she continued, "who humbled himself by descending from the royal throne into the Virgin's womb, wanting to appear despised, needy, and poor,[65] Francis, too, renounced the wealth and luxury of his father's house for a life of poverty. I, too—like Francis—have renounced my noble inheritance. And we did this in order to follow in the footsteps of the poor, lesser Christ. This is why I am here."

Sister Angela was there, too, and she smiled as she listened to Clare's beautiful words. *Perhaps there was nothing wrong with this peculiar woman*, she thought to herself. *On the contrary, everything seems right with her*"

Clare continued, "Remember what Our Lord said, 'The Son of man came not to be served but to serve, and to give his life as a ransom for many,' and, 'If I then, your Lord and Teacher, have washed your feet, you also ought to wash one another's feet.' My feet have been washed. Now I am here to wash the feet of others. This is why I am here: to serve."

The sisters sat there amazed, as they had never met anyone like Clare before. She spoke with the accent and airs of a noblewoman, yet she betrayed no conceit or ostentation. They had heard the words of Scripture she quoted, but never before had they met someone whose way of life matched them so closely. Clare's words were backed up with her life; she had actually done what the words instructed.

"My sisters, remember always the words of Scripture: 'Humble yourselves therefore under the mighty hand of God, that in due time he may exalt you.' Let these words guide you always in your work and your life. Be humble! Never doubt that 'the kingdom of heaven is yours!' Your dignity is in Christ: you are all Ladies! True Ladies! For you, too, are as a bride 'adorned with her jewels.'"

By now some of the sisters had tears in their eyes, as no one had ever spoken to them the way Clare did. Clare, too, felt a sisterly bond with the simple *conversae* there in San Paolo.

Yet, despite Clare's newfound joy, her stay at San Paolo had been chosen strategically. The Monastery of San Paolo boasted numerous papal privileges. No feudal power could exact tithes against it; the diocesan bishop was forbidden to discipline their chapel; and they could receive free women from secular life despite objections from their families.

However, it also had one other unique privilege. A papal order was in force prohibiting outsiders from entering the cloister. As such, the San Paolo monastery offered broad rights of asylum and prevented the threat of violence. No one would dare seek to remove a consecrated nun from such a papal convent against her will. For to do so would incur excommunication.

And this would prove to be the first papal privilege Clare would need in her new life.

> *Saint Francis immediately led her to the church of San Paolo to remain there until the Most High would provide another place.*
>
> LEGEND 4:8

7

KNIGHTS AND NUNS

Many waters cannot quench love, neither can floods drown it. If a man offered for love all the wealth of his house, it would be utterly scorned.

SONG OF SOLOMON 8:7

SISTER Angela raced down the corridor toward the quarters of the *choristae*. She was terrified as she shouted, "Mother Abbess! Mother Abbess!" Startled, the choir nuns came out of their apartments where they had been studying Scripture. They stared at one another alarmed at what might be happening.

Sister Angela burst into the abbess's study yelling for her to come quickly. Appalled at her indecorous entrance, Abbess Sibilia reprimanded her. "What is the cause of this commotion, Sister?" she demanded to know.

"Mother Abbess, there are men outside on horses armed with swords. They are banging on the door, demanding to come inside!" she stammered.

"Donna Prioress, come with me," ordered the abbess as she promptly arose and walked swiftly toward the entrance of the monastery. As she walked hurriedly down the corridor approaching the main entrance, the prioress struggled to keep up with her. As they neared the door, the abbess could hear pounding on the door and commotion outside. The choir nuns watched frightfully at the threshold of their apartment doors as the scene unfolded.

The abbess slid open the small grilled access panel in the upper part of the door. She looked around and assessed the situation. There were about a dozen men. Some were on horseback while others were armed with swords at their sides. They were noblemen and knights.

She looked at the men's faces and gazed into their eyes. She was good at reading men and knowing what was in their souls. She watched them for a moment as they jested amongst themselves irreverently. She did not like what she saw.

"What is the meaning of this?" she roared above their strident voices. Her powerful voice startled Sister Angela, who had never heard her abbess speak in such a way, petite as she was.

"You have someone in there who belongs to us!" screamed one of them back at her. "We demand you open this door and hand her over to us!"

The abbess responded again forcefully, "How dare you come here making such crude demands—and during Holy Week no less! You are standing on holy ground, which you are desecrating with your war horses and daggers. In the name of religion and all that is holy, I command you to end this mischief and depart from this monastery at once!"

"If you do not open this door right now, we will break it down and take Lady Clare out of here by force!" one of the knights yelled back. At this, they became even more excited, and some started yelling obscenities at her while others blasphemed the Virgin Mary and the saints.

The abbess slid the small panel shut and thought for a moment. Usually thugs like these could be handled fairly easily by employing the fear of God, she thought to herself. However, these men were particularly disgraceful. She could summon the armed guards . . . However, these knights were so agitated that she feared risking bloodshed right there at the threshold of her monastery. She thought again for a moment. Then she knew exactly what to do.

She spoke calmly and assertively to the prioress, "Bring me my crozier." The prioress wavered and started to object. Sibilia, however, cut her short and repeated her order even more decisively, "I said for you to bring me my crozier this instant!"

As the prioress ran back down the corridor, the horrified choir nuns returned inside their apartments and bolted the doors. Meanwhile, the threats and curses outside the monastery only grew louder. Sister Angela stood there terrified, staring at her abbess and wondering what she was about to do.

When the prioress returned with her crozier, Abbess Sibilia ordered the extern sister to unbolt the door. Sister Angela looked at her in shock. The abbess nodded steadily to encourage her. The frightened lay sister obeyed, and with trembling hands, slowly unlocked the two thick metal bolts, slid them open, and then pulled open the heavy door. She then hid behind it.

The abbess then did something she never did: she broke the bounds of the monastic cloister and walked through the door. She took several steps toward the furious armed men and then held up her crozier. The men, taken by surprise, were immediately silenced. Standing there with her crozier lifted on high before the small army of knights, she looked like Moses with his staff raised before the Amalekites.

"In the name of Jesus Christ, I command you to leave this monastery!" she thundered.

The sight of this undersized elderly nun standing before them in full religious garb with crozier in hand disarmed the men. Immediately, their demeanor changed and they settled down.

"Mother Abbess," began one of them in a now tranquil voice. It was Clare's uncle, Monaldo, still seated on his horse. "You have a relative of ours who is staying inside your monastery. We request that you send her out at once. She does not have our blessing to be here."

"Very well, she does not have your blessing to be here," responded the abbess, unfazed by her vulnerability before the men. "But she has the blessing of our ecclesiastical lord, Bishop Guido, to be here! She has the blessing of Almighty God to be here! And she has MY blessing to be here! I can assure you that she will NOT leave this monastery!"

This only infuriated Monaldo. His face turning red, he dismounted from his horse and walked slowly and menacingly toward the abbess. He was a hulk of a man for his time, roughly six feet tall in stature. With enraged eyes, he stared down at the elderly nun half his height before him. He had used his size and this same piercing expression countless times in his life. It often worked to his advantage on the battlefield or at the negotiating table. Surely it would work on this little nun.

Placing his hand over the handle of his sword, he leaned down toward the abbess and lowered his face to the same level as hers. He enunciated his words carefully as he said,

"You will stand aside as I enter this monastery, find my niece, and drag her out of here by her hair."

The abbess was undeterred. She returned his stare and even took a step closer to him. Speaking in an equally articulate voice, she said, "If you do such a thing, I assure you that this very day I will dispatch an emissary to the Holy See of Peter in Rome. And he will speak directly with the Holy Father himself, the Vicar of Christ, Lord Pope Innocent III." She noticed Monaldo wince. She then paused for a moment to let the gravity of her words sink in.

As she spoke, she lifted herself up on her toes moving her face even closer to Monaldo's. "And he will state to the pontiff precisely what you have done today.

"My emissary will enlighten the pontiff as to how you have committed sacrilege this day: that you brazenly and mercilessly violated the sanctity of the holy cloister of this sacred papal monastery, San Paolo of the Handmaidens." She paused again and moved even closer to him. By now her face was so close to Monaldo's that she could feel his warm breath on her face. It was rancid.

"And you will be held in interdict and subject to excommunication. And then you will lose your knightly and noble titles and all you hold dear. And I will be waiting here when you crawl back to me begging for mercy."

Abbess Sibilia remained immobile between the open door to her monastery and her adversary. She stared him down, knowing full well he would back down.

Finally, Monaldo scoffed. He leaned forward even closer to the nun, their noses almost touching, and said with a scowl, "Woman, we will be back! I promise you that!" He then turned around, mounted his horse, and ordered the others to leave. And with that, the men galloped off on the Campiglione Road back to Assisi.

Abbess Sibilia remained in the doorway until the men disappeared out of sight. When they were gone, she returned inside the enclosure of the monastery, whereafter Sister Angela quickly shut and barred the door.

The abbess said to Sister Angela, "Get Donna Clare and bring her to my study right away." After the lay sister ran off, the abbess rested her back against the door for a moment. Her heart was pounding. She took several deep breaths and recomposed herself. She looked over at the prioress and exclaimed, "*Deo Gratias*! (Thanks be to God!)" Then the two walked quickly back to her study.

When Sister Angela recounted to Clare what happened, the former noblewoman ran ahead of the lay sister all the way to the abbess's study. She threw the door open abruptly and exclaimed, "Mother Abbess, forgive me for what happened!"

"Donna Clare, your relatives came for you with violence and ferocity," responded the abbess, unmindful of her inappropriate entrance. "I had anticipated a confrontation, but not one so fierce. They comported themselves as true thugs. I was able to prevent them from desecrating this monastery and committing sacrilege only through most astute maneuvering."

"Reverend Abbess," replied Clare, "they will return. I am sure of it."

"I know they will. In fact, I called you here to tell you that I fear for your presence here. It is no longer safe for you to remain with us. We must communicate all to Lord Guido and negotiate another place for you to stay. At once."

"Mother Abbess, that will not be necessary. When they return, I will go to them and speak with them," Clare said.

The abbess looked over at the prioress with concern and considered Clare's intentions for a moment. She then shook her head and said, "No, Donna Clare, I will not allow this. Such an encounter will put you at too great a risk."

Though Clare had not professed vows under her obedience, the abbess nonetheless took Clare's custody just as seriously as if she were any of the professed nuns in her monastery. She was afraid for her. Yet her desire to protect Clare was not just as abbess. It was instinctive, as a mother.

"Mother Abbess, I knew they would come," said Clare. "But I am ready. I am not afraid. I trust in the Lord. God will not allow me to be harmed. I know it."

Though all her instincts told her to deny Clare's request, something, Someone, moved Sibilia to permit it. She knew Clare was right. She had to face her relatives, and the abbess could not intervene. Abbess Sibilia looked at Clare with maternal compassion and granted her request.

The next day, the men did indeed come back. However, their demeanor had softened. They arrived unarmed and left their horses far from the entrance to the monastery. Monaldo rapped the knocker gently on the wooden door.

When Sister Angela opened the upper speaking panel, Clare's uncle spoke through the grille, "Please call on your Mother Abbess and tell her that we wish to speak with our relative, Lady Clare. We will not use force. We only wish to plead with her. I beg you." Sister Angela did as Monaldo requested. The abbess, in turn, told her to bring Clare to her study.

When Clare arrived, she was peaceful and more radiant than ever. She told the abbess that she wished to meet her relatives in the church. The abbess consented. She told Sister Angela to tell the men to go into the church, where they would meet with Clare. She then accompanied Clare into the church through the choir stalls from within the monastery.

When the men arrived through the front door of the church, Clare was already there kneeling before the altar praying beneath the crucifix. The abbess remained in the choir to the side of the altar where she could see Clare. As she was within the cloister, she was not visible to anyone in the church except Clare. The abbess watched her and prayed for her safety all the while.

"Clare!" shouted Monaldo from the back of the church as soon as he saw his niece. Remaining before the altar, she stood up, turned around, and faced the men. He was shocked, as all the men were. Clare, his niece—who only days earlier wore fine gowns and jewels—was now barefoot and vested in a peasant's tunic with a religious veil over her head. They were stunned at her transformation and stood there speechless.

Clare's father broke the silence.[66] He shoved his older brother out of the way and cried, "Clare, what have you done? What has happened to my silver dove? Why have you done such a thing?" His desperation was evident as he spoke, trembling. Clare, however, remained silent.

"You've broken my heart," he said. "And you broke your mother's heart, too," he added slyly. "I should tell you that she cannot sleep at night. You know her health is not good . . . And this is only making it worse. Your sisters, too, are devastated, as are the ladies-in-wait . . . and the neighbors. We're all distraught."

Clare had anticipated such lies and conniving by her relatives. However, she did not expect how she would feel. In truth, her heart was breaking, too. For the man standing before her begging was her earthly lord and father.

As he stood before her pleading, Clare could not stop the memories from flooding through her mind. She recalled when she was a girl and her father used to throw her up in the air, how she would giggle and squeal with delight. With his large hands and strong arms, she felt consoled as he embraced her tightly. She would gaze into his eyes where she saw strength, intelligence, confidence, and graciousness. He was a powerful and valiant knight who had always loved her, protected her, and provided for her.

As she looked at him now, however, Clare discerned something she had not noticed before. She saw it first in his eyes. Whereas they used to twinkle, they now showed signs of weariness. When he moved about, he seemed fatigued, and his once-broad shoulders were now stooped. His face was worn, too, and his color faded. The creases in his forehead were now more pronounced, and his face was thinner. His voice, once poised and assured, was now raspy. Her father was becoming an old man.

"What has come over you, Clare?" Favarone continued. "Have you entered religion? Here? Then why are you dressed that way?" Every fiber in her natural being compelled her to go to him, to care for him and ease his suffering. For up to that point, he had been her lord. Yet, though she wanted to go to him, she resisted.

"Clare, we had been meaning to tell you something," her earthly father continued. "Lord Ranieri has asked for your hand in marriage. You know him—the son of Count Bernardo. You've known him since your childhood, and I know you are fond of him. And we have given our consent. I am sure you will be pleased with this arrangement. You will have lands and castles. Our families will both be united and stronger . . . And happy, too."[67]

Then the others interrupted him and began to implore her to come home. Some told her how she was making a mistake while others offered advice. They tried to flatter her with still more promises of wealth and worldly privileges. They told her that people were speaking badly about her and that she was ruining their family's reputation. They said that what she was doing was unsuitable to her class and no one had ever done such a thing. But still Clare remained silent.

"Why do you remain silent? Speak, girl!" commanded Clare's father.

By now, Monaldo finally lost his patience. "Girl, you will come with us now or we will drag you out of here by your hair!" he threatened as he pushed himself back in front of his brother.

"I will not leave this monastery!" Clare finally bellowed, breaking her silence. Her forceful voice, normally soft and gentle, startled the abbess. But Clare's refusal only agitated Monaldo all the more. He started toward her.

To the abbess, Clare appeared as one of the young virgin martyrs before their persecutors—Agatha, Lucy, Agnes, or Cecilia. Abbess Sibilia readied herself to go to her. She wanted so strongly to go to her, to place herself between her and the men threatening her.

Before she had the chance to, however, Clare did something completely unexpected. Surprising everyone in the church, she grabbed the altar cloth with one hand and removed her veil with the other. Monaldo froze. So did all the men.

Clare—their lovely daughter, niece, or cousin—stood there before them with her head razed. She was completely bald, all her hair shorn. Her appearance was hideous and dreadful to them. Clare's father staggered forward and fell to a knee. He felt as if he had been knocked off his horse as during a joust. His beautiful daughter now seemed sickly, as if she had some disease.

The abbess watched in astonishment as Clare stood before the altar gazing upward into the distance at something, Someone, no one else could see. Motionless and expressionless, she appeared to her as a living Byzantine icon, illuminating and radiating a mysterious energy.

She turned to her father and addressed him gently, "Sir Favarone, son of Offreduccio, grandson of Bernardino, knight and Major of Assisi. For eighteen years you have been my lord, my master, my love. You have been my father, and I will forever give thanks to God for the life and love you have given me. I have always loved you, and I will continue to always love you.[68]

"However, I can no longer give you my obedience," she continued. "For you are no longer my lord or my master. Now I am following a new Lord, a new Love, and a different Father. What my spiritual father, Francis, said to his earthly father some years ago, I now say to you: I, too, have but one

Father, 'Our Father who art in heaven.'" At the mention of Francis's name, a murmur went up among the men.

While she spoke, tears began to well up in her eyes, as well as in her father's. She was able to do what she was doing only with the strength God provided. For Clare was no longer talking, thinking, or reasoning as a child. Instead, she was of age and had put away childish things. Only through grace was she able to look beyond her earthly father and keep her gaze fixed on the Father who was infinitely more powerful, consoling, and wise.

For this was, in effect, a struggle of wills. And there were three involved: the heavenly Father's, Clare's, and her worldly father's. God had willed Clare to begin a new life, and she accepted it. But Favarone did not. Thus, the dramatic conflict unfolding was not Clare's choice: it was the consequence of her decision to follow the will of her heavenly Father and not that of her worldly father.

She then turned her attention to the rest of her relatives. "The life you are all calling me to comes from my earthly father. But now I am following a heavenly Father. And my heavenly Father is calling me to a different life: not one of worldly privileges and promises, but one of heavenly privileges and promises—that of poverty."

Clare's father understood in that moment that it was over. He knew that no amount of persuasion or coaxing would have any effect on her decision. His daughter was like him—resolute and determined. She was the daughter of a knight, and she would fight for this with everything she had. Her balded head—the tonsure—was the sign of his daughter's permanent consecration and entrance into religion. It was as if she had a wedding band on her hand.

There was nothing that could be done. Without a word, he stood, turned, and left. The others followed him.

After they left, Clare withdrew from the altar and returned within the monastery. The abbess remained in the choir stalls, amazed. It was at that moment when she realized that this was no ordinary young woman staying there in her good monastery. She thought of Scripture: "Do not think that I have come to bring peace on earth; I have not come to bring peace, but a sword. For I have come to set a man against his father, and a daughter against her mother, and a daughter-in-law against her mother-in-law; and a man's foes will be those of his own household" (Mt 10:34–36).

Clare stayed at San Paolo for a little while longer, during which time some of the men came back several more times. They tried to persuade her with more bribes and manipulations to leave the monastery. However, when they finally realized Clare was resolute, they stopped coming to San Paolo. And they never came back.

When Clare was certain she was safe from them, it was time to leave. She knew she could not stay there in San Paolo permanently. The noble and feudal ways of San Paolo were not consistent with the religious form of life she felt called to. Clare wanted to live as a Franciscan. She wanted to rely only on the providence of God, not on the security of the feudal monastery. As a Franciscan woman, she wanted only one privilege: poverty. Therefore, with the intervention of Francis, it was decided that Clare would leave and go to another place.

Before Clare left, she had one final audience with the abbess in which she communicated her intentions and explained how she intended to follow Francis in the footsteps of Christ in poverty. With the prioress standing at her side, Sibilia listened to Clare. This time, however, she did so with admiration.

"Donna Clare . . . *Sister* Clare, I believe I was wrong about you," said the abbess. At this, the prioress raised her eyebrows, unable to mask her surprise at her superior's rare admission of errant judgment.

"I admire you for your remarkable courage and determination, which I have personally witnessed," the abbess continued. "You are truly an extraordinary young woman. You are tenacious and you are, indeed, guided by the Spirit. I wish you well in all your endeavors." Clare thanked her for her words.

"Now, you may go," said the abbess somewhat coldly as she turned her attention to a ledger on the desk next to her.

Clare turned and walked toward the door, opened by Sister Angela. As she did so, she was feeling gratitude for all the abbess had done for her. The way the abbess had placed herself between Clare and her aggressors was an example that would remain with her forever. As she passed through the door, however, the abbess looked up from her ledger, watching her leave. Suddenly, something welled up inside her. With a twinkle in her eyes, she said unexpectedly, "Clare, come back here."

Clare turned around and went to the abbess and kneeled before her. The abbess looked directly into her eyes, traced the cross on Clare's forehead, embraced her, and said, "You will always have a home at San Paolo—certainly with the *choristae* . . . or even with the *conversae*." Clare was moved by her tenderness. Though Clare was not sure, she thought she saw a tear begin to well up from within the abbess's eyes. The abbess, however, quickly turned away and composed herself.

After a moment, she turned back and said, "Sister Clare, there is something else I feel I must tell you." Clare listened attentively as the wise old abbess placed her hands on her shoulders, looked deep into her eyes, and said, "Francis and the brothers are men, Clare. We, my daughter, are women. Therefore, as you make your way in this world, and in our Church, 'be wise as a serpent and innocent as doves.' And may God accompany you always."

Clare thanked her again. She felt consoled by her support but also a little troubled by her admonition. For the abbess knew the ways of the world . . . and of the Church.

Clare then left the study and walked down the long corridor with Sister Angela toward the main door. The extern lay sister said to her, "Clare, you are indeed a lady—whether 'in the world' or 'in religion'—in heart and soul. And you have been true to your namesake, a real light to us. Thank you for everything you have done for us here."

"And you, Sister Angela," replied Clare, "are truly an 'angel.' May God bless you." She then traced the cross on Sister Angela's forehead and embraced her. Sister Angela opened the door, where Francis was waiting outside. And with that, Clare left San Paolo of the Abbesses.

But after the news reached Clare's relatives, they condemned with a broken heart the deed and proposal of the virgin and, banding together as one, they ran to the place, attempting to obtain what they could not. They employed violent force, poisonous advice, and flattering promises, trying to persuade her to give up such a worthless deed that was unbecoming to her class and without precedence in her family. But, taking hold of the altar cloths, she bared her tonsured head, maintaining that she would in no way be torn away from the service of Christ. With the increasing violence of her relatives, her spirit grew and her love—provoked by injuries—provided strength. So for many days, even though she endured an obstacle in the way of the Lord and her own relatives opposed her proposal of holiness, her spirit did not crumble and her fervor did not diminish. Instead, amid words and deeds of hatred, she molded her spirit anew in hope until her relatives, turning back, were quiet.

LEGEND 4:8–9

8

SANT'ANGELO IN PANZO

Scarcely had I passed them, when I found him whom my soul loves. I held him, and would not let him go.

SONG OF SOLOMON 3:4

TOGETHER with Brothers Bernard and Philip, Francis accompanied Clare from the monastery of San Paolo to her next destination.[69] The friars walked with their sister along the Campiglione Road until they reached Assisi. Before entering the city gate by the men's Benedictine monastery of San Pietro, they turned right and walked downhill on the road toward St. Mary of the Angels. At the Via Antiqua, the "ancient road", they turned left. Then, at the Valecchie Road, they turned left again and walked back up to the Moiano city gate, which Clare had slipped through not long before.

As Francis walked with his followers, they were like Jesus on the road to Emmaus with his disciples. Perhaps Francis shared stories from Scripture with his brothers and sister. Or maybe they stopped along the way to break bread together. Surely their hearts were burning within them while he spoke to them (cf. Lk 24:32). For as they journeyed together, they rejoiced at having shunned the trappings of the institutional monastic setting for a more authentic experience, embracing the uncertainties of the world together with the certainties of God's love.

As Clare and the brothers continued walking, the remarkable beauty of the great Spoleto Valley struck Clare and she marveled at the wonders of the world. That basin, formed over millennia by the Clitumnus, Topino, Chiascio, and the mighty Tiber Rivers, was striking. Clare admired the land and stones she was walking on, the olive trees and wild vegetation on either side of the road, and the mountains on all sides of the valley. She inhaled the earthy aroma of the damp soil and wondered at the fragrance of the fig trees, lavender, and wild mint. Clare, like Francis, loved natural creation. God's created world was truly beautiful, she thought to herself, and she praised God when she was out and about in it.[70]

When passersby noticed Francis and Clare together, they stopped and stared. Some gasped. They had all heard the rumors: Clare, the beautiful daughter of one of the wealthiest noblemen of Assisi, had entered religion as a follower of Francis, the son of one of the wealthiest merchants of Assisi. Now they knew it was true; they were seeing it with their own eyes. There they were. Clare was walking along with Francis and the brothers.

Those who were pious and knew of their holiness felt joy in their hearts at seeing Francis and Clare together, and they made the sign of the cross as they passed by. They knew the two would do great things for the city of Assisi and for the Church. Others thought the whole affair strange. *Where were they going? What were they up to?* they thought to themselves.

Some townspeople, however—particularly those averse to religion—imagined lewd things. Some, in fact, yelled out obscenities and made vulgar gestures as Francis and Clare passed by. The brothers promptly rebuked them firmly, but fraternally, for speaking and acting in such a way.

Clare, however, pulled her hood over her head and prayed quietly for those whose hearts needed healing and conversion. She kept her eyes guarded and returned neither the comments nor the stares of the townsfolk. By now she was well acquainted with making a "monastery" of her spirit, and she had custody over her eyes and spirit. The rudeness of the world did not affect her as it did others.

Occasionally, she glanced back up at Assisi. Though only a short time had passed since her departure from "the world," things seemed so different to her now. Assisi—with all its wickedness and corruption—had not changed. But she had. She knew that she could do the most good for Assisi where she was going. And her heart beamed with joy at the thought.

The penitents walked along the trail that flanked the city walls and made their way to the other side of Assisi. When they passed by the gate next to the little church of San Giorgio, Clare thought of St. George and how he slew dragons. Neither Clare nor Francis had any idea that they would both be temporarily buried in that little church until large grandiose basilicas were built to entomb them. Francis's would be on the other side of the city while Clare would remain right there next to St. George.

The penitents then took the road up the slope of Mount Subasio that led to Spello. As they ambled up the San Savino road through the countryside, they saluted the shepherds driving their flocks of sheep and cows up the mountain to feast on its spring herbage. Francis had trodden that trail many times, as it was the same mule track he took up to the caves known as the Carceri (the cells) where he went frequently for prayer and solitude.

But that day, he was not going to prayer. He was accompanying Clare to the next destination on her earthly pilgrimage: Sant'Angelo in Panzo.[71]

Panzo was located before the Carceri caves in the plains down the ravine (known locally as the *fosso*) that formed at the top of Mount Subasio and extended all the way down to the valley near Rivotorto. Full of underground springs, Panzo was an important source of water for Assisi, as it had been since ancient times. It had once, long ago in fact, provided water even to the Roman temple of Minerva.[72]

Yet presently of interest to Clare and Francis was the little church there dedicated to St. Michael the Archangel and the community of penitential women living around it. Francis thought that Clare would be better off there in the community in Panzo, as it was a little further from Assisi than San Paolo and would hopefully keep her safer from the clutches of her family.

But for Clare, Panzo was important because it was more closely aligned with the religious form of life she was seeking. The penitential women there were not noblewomen, and its structure was less formal than San Paolo. There were no distinctions between *choristae* or *conversae*, no dowries, no rents or land ownership. Instead, a simple group of women lived together there in prayer, service, and work. Clare would be happier there.[73]

Clare was more contented with her new community. For she knew that she could not live the spiritual life alone; she had to have sisters. The Franciscan form of life she was seeking could not be lived alone. Just as Francis had to have brothers to have fraternity, she, too, had to have sisters for fraternity—or more properly, sorority.

And the next day, the first one came. It was now two weeks since her "conversion"—when she left her father's household.[74]

Clare was at prayer when she looked up. There, standing before her was Catherine, her younger sister in the world. She was her closest companion, her intimate confidant. Now Catherine had made her decision: she would be more than Clare's sister in blood, she would be her sister now in religion. Clare was jubilant and could not contain her joy.

However, even though Good Friday had passed and the churches were now celebrating the liturgical season of Easter and rebirth, Catherine's passion was just about to begin. Clare's encounters with her relatives were not over. They were coming back, and they were more furious than ever.

Back in Assisi, Pacifica had been nervously eyeing the castle from her window across the square of San Rufino. She knew what was coming, but there was nothing she could do. She wanted to go to them so badly. But she could not. For now.

And then it happened. The next day, a dozen men rushed furiously out of the castle. Pacifica watched helplessly as they mounted their horses and galloped past the fountain in the square, disappearing on the road up past the ancient Roman theater and sarcophagus toward Mount Subasio.

Pacifica ran to the household chapel and fell to her knees in prayer. "God help them!" she shouted out.

While Clare was inside the enclosure of Panzo talking about spiritual things with Catherine, they arrived. And just as they had done two weeks earlier in San Paolo, the men of their family worked to connive their way into the community. The sisters of Panzo, however, were poorer and simpler than the women of San Paolo, and the porter sister naively let them in.

They went straight to Catherine. "Girl, you will come with us now!" demanded Monaldo.

"No! I will not leave my sister, Clare," Catherine answered decisively. The men became enraged and ferocious.

"Girl, your sister has already dishonored our entire family by fooling us and leaving in the middle of the night and joining that ragamuffin, Francis!" yelled Monaldo. "Her trickery and deceit has made us the laughingstock of Assisi! And now she has deceived you! You will not stay here! We will decide where you go and what you do. And you are coming with us now!"

Here in Panzo, the men were in a much better position to assert their will, as Panzo did not boast the same papal privileges as San Paolo. One of the men wearing heavy riding gloves violently back-handed Catherine, bloodying her and knocking her nearly unconscious. The others dragged her out of the monastery.

Clare watched in horror as her sister did her best to fend off the sharp blows while they pulled her down the mountain and ripped her hair out by the roots. She ran into the chapel and interceded to the Lord on her sister's behalf.

Suddenly, Catherine's body became so heavy that the men could no longer carry her.

At this, her uncle, Monaldo, could not contain his fury. "What's wrong with you men?" he cried as he clenched his fist, raised his hand, and readied himself to deliver the final blow. Clare, at prayer, could spiritually see what was happening, and she prayed even harder. At that moment, Clare's uncle was suddenly seized by a horrible pain, and he was unable to move his hand.

"Ahhhh!" cried Monaldo, as he realized that something out of the ordinary was happening. Finally, he came to his senses and looked at his niece there on the side of the mountain, bleeding and bruised, her hair strewn across the thickets and brush. Uncharacteristically, a sense of compassion overtook him and he felt pity for his niece. He then mounted his horse and commanded the other men to do the same. They returned to Assisi the same number as when they had left.

This was Clare's first miracle.[75]

Clare ran to her sister and brought her back into the community and tended to her wounds. Francis heard the news and came immediately. As he had done with Clare in the Church of St. Mary of the Angels, he ensured this would not happen again. There, in the church dedicated to St. Michael the Archangel, he cut off Catherine's hair, giving her the tonsure with his own hand. Now the men would not come back.[76]

Because of Catherine's suffering, Clare and Francis changed her name. She would now be called Agnes. From then on, Clare's sister would bear the name of the young Roman virgin-martyr of the Church who also suffered for her love of Christ. But more importantly, she now bore the name of the Lamb of God, Christ. And Agnes would fully embrace the inner meaning of her namesake. For she would testify with her life to the Lord's preference for humility, minority, and poverty—the Lamb who makes himself poor and humble so that people would become rich in divinity.[77]

Francis then told Clare that it was time for her to move again. The arrangements for her final home were ready. Clare, for her part, was ready to go, too. Her brief stay in Panzo was a step in the right direction toward the way of life she was called to. But, like San Paolo, Panzo was not intended to be her permanent home. She was not at peace there either.

Perhaps Panzo, despite its more penitential practices and simplicity, was still too institutionalized for Clare. Or perhaps it was too well-endowed for the voluntary poverty she wished to fully embrace. Unfortunately, history has left us with too vague a picture to understand clearly why Clare went to Panzo, or why she left.

The *Legend* summarized her entire experience in Panzo in one cryptically brief sentence: "After a few days [in San Paolo], she went to the Church of San Angelo in Panzo, where her mind was not completely at peace, so that, at the advice of Francis, she moved."[78] Clare and Agnes's younger sister, Beatrice, was the only ancient source to ever name the place, but she gave even less information, testifying only that Francis and the two brothers "took her to the Church of Sant'Angelo of Panzo where she stayed for a little time."[79]

Despite her lack of peace, surely Clare was grateful to the sisters of Panzo for her brief sojourn there. And the women of Sant'Angelo in Panzo were certainly struck by the two holy sisters who stayed with them, even if only for a short time. Later, in 1238, they would be, in fact, one of the first women's communities to adopt Clare's way of life—the "Rule of the Damianites" as it was called.

After giving Sister Agnes the tonsure, Francis accompanied the two sisters—in blood and now in religion—to their final home: the place of the prophecy.

> *Hearing that Agnes had gone off to Clare, twelve men, burning with anger and hiding outwardly their evil intent, ran to [the church of San Angelo in Panzo], and pretended to make a peaceful entrance. . . . When she responded that she did not want to leave her sister, Clare, one of the knights in a fierce mood ran toward her and, without sparing blows and kicks, tried to drag her away by her hair while the others pushed her and lifted her in their arms. . . . Clare prostrated herself in prayer with tears, begged that her sister would be given constancy of mind and that the strength of humans would be overcome by divine power. Suddenly, in fact, Agnes's body lying on the ground seemed so heavy that the men, many as there were, exerted all their energy and were not able to carry her beyond a certain stream. . . . Then Lord Monaldo, her enraged uncle, intended to strike her a lethal blow, but an awful pain suddenly struck the hand he had raised and for a long time the anguish of pain afflicted it. . . . Then Blessed Francis cut off her hair with his own hand and directed her together with her sister in the way of the Lord."*
>
> LEGEND 16:25

9

SAN DAMIANO: ENCLOSED AND OPEN

A garden locked is my sister, my bride, a garden locked, a fountain sealed.

SONG OF SOLOMON 4:12

AS Francis walked his two sisters back down the mountain from Panzo toward Assisi, they moved slowly as Agnes's condition permitted. As they walked, Clare marveled at God's magnificent creation all around her. She delighted in the giant warm blue sky, the magnificent valley, and the sweet Umbrian air. She marveled at the fragrant wild herbs and the singing larks darting playfully to and fro in the sky. She admired the spring wildflowers and the slight silver-green olive trees in the inviting orchards. It was like a magnificent garden—as if all creation were welcoming Clare to her new home.

At the gate by San Giorgio, they took the road to the left and started downhill toward Clare's next and final residence: San Damiano. Francis knew this road well, as it continued past San Damiano toward the crooked stream known as Rivotorto. There Francis had lived with his first eleven brothers in animal sheds until three years earlier. The road then continued on to the village of Spina where

Francis's father owned property and where he had rebuilt another little church known as San Pietrignano.

In a short time, they came to a small shrine dedicated to St. Felicianus. Around the beginning of the third century, he was one of the first of the ancient evangelizers to bring Christianity to Assisi. According to local lore, the Good News he brought was rejected, and he was expelled from Assisi on that very hillside. So he left and went on to nearby Foligno where he started a community and became bishop. Later, after he refused to sacrifice to the Roman gods during the persecutions of Emperor Decius, he was arrested and, despite his elderly age, severely tortured and killed.

Now Christianity was the predominant religion not just in Umbria but in all of Italy, and Felicianus was venerated as the patron saint of Foligno. Indeed, the great cathedral built in his honor and name was visible in the distance to the south. Clare looked over at her sister, Agnes, hobbling and limping along. *Most people may be Catholic today*, she thought to herself, *but faithfulness to the Gospel still had a price.*

A few paces after the martyr's shrine stood a tomb of a different sort; there was an ancient Roman sarcophagus. Though ruined now, this sepulcher had once depicted all the achievements its occupant had accomplished during his lifetime in ornately decorated marble bas-relief. In antiquity, the Roman nobility often put their tombs next to the important roads in and out of town. Not believing in an afterlife, they wanted the world to see and know the deeds they had accomplished in this life.

Clare considered the two memorials for a moment—one dedicated to a saintly martyr and the other to a worldly pagan. She reflected on them: the first suffered in this world and was willing to renounce for Christ his life in the hope of glory in the next; the other, instead, lived a life of esteem and honor in this world with no hope for the next. How different were their attitudes to life . . . and to death.

The three then continued down the hillside, which soon began to descend steeply. Soon, they reached their destination: a small rustic church dedicated to the second of the two physician brothers Cosmos and Damian.[80]

When Clare looked up at her new home, she was jubilant. The little church was made simply of cream-colored stone, quarried from nearby Subasio. The plain, non-decorative stone façade of the Romanesque church was perfect in its bare and stark beauty. It blended seamlessly and harmoniously with the blue sky above and the natural green around it. Next to the church were several huts made of wood and straw. It was just like the poor places where Francis dwelled—Rivotorto and St. Mary of the Angels.[81]

In ancient times, there had been a pagan shrine there to honor perhaps the Roman god Mithra or Sol Invictus (Unconquerable Sun). But after the local populace converted to Christianity, the temple was transformed into a church. It was now known by the locals simply as San Damiano.

When Clare arrived at San Damiano, she was only eighteen years old. Yet she sensed in her heart that she would live out the rest of her years there. Indeed, over the next forty-two years, she would leave its small church and little enclosure only on the rarest of occasions. But this was not penance for Clare. Because within the small grounds of San Damiano lay the greatest treasures and desires of her heart.

The moment she set foot within the little church and enclosure something stirred powerfully from the depths of her being. Whereas most would have felt loneliness there, Clare experienced sweetness. Instead of emptiness or barrenness, the stillness of San Damiano was, to her, great delight. Its poverty filled her soul with a fullness and joy she had never before experienced. It was like the Psalm: "You anoint my head with oil, / my cup overflows. / Surely goodness and mercy shall follow me / all the days of my life; / and I shall dwell in the house of the LORD / for ever" (Ps 23:5–6).

To Clare, the little church was a majestic cathedral, its humble cloister an impregnable fortress. The enclosure was as a watchtower: it guarded her heart and protected her there within. In San Damiano were completeness and realization, kindness and goodness. She felt wiser and stronger, whole and fulfilled. She knew she would never leave. She was home.

In this, Clare's vocation was not the same as that of Francis. Clare would not live itinerantly or accompany Francis and the brothers out in the world. She would not preach the Gospel, beg for bread, or serve the sick on the outside. Instead, she would live the ideals of the Franciscan movement within. Her Franciscan vocation would be "veiled" within the intimacy and tenderness of the cloister. And this enclosed way of life was something she embraced freely and wholeheartedly from the beginning.[82]

The religious cloister was certainly not new in religious life. It traced its origins back to the ancient way of life of the desert fathers and mothers of antiquity. For the men and women of the desert, the communal life within the penitential cloister was considered the best place to counter the sin of Adam and live in the grace of Christ through poverty, chastity, and obedience.

In later times, St. Benedict brought order and stability to communities of hermits and recluses with the great Benedictine Rule, leading to the formalization of monasticism in the West. Only recently, in fact, were men experimenting with religious life outside the stability of the monastery on a large scale. In truth, it was Francis and the other mendicants of that era who were just beginning to live their "cloister" out in the world as they preached to the people in the newly urbanized cities.

But Francis and the brothers were men. Clare, however, was a woman. And she was a woman of her times. And the times were not conducive for women—especially religious women—to be outside. Therefore, Clare's form of life—like virtually all religious women of her day—would be lived within the cloister.

Despite the universal practice of the cloister for women, times were changing in the Church. In the twelfth and early thirteenth centuries, new ways of life for religious women were developing. And they were less structured and ordered than the stable way of life within "regular" monasticism.

Instead of living in monasteries with thick walls, these women lived in simpler buildings called "hospices" or hermitages. They sought to imitate Christ by devoting themselves to the poor, serving the sick in nearby hospitals, and practicing other religious devotions. Known as Beguines in Flanders and Belgium, in Italy they were called *bizoche*. Clare was surely familiar with these movements and possibly had contact with them.[83]

Indeed, while it is clear that Clare embraced the cloister, she did so more subtly and never accepted its most stringent practices. In its most severe form, religious life in many traditional monasteries was centered on the notion of not just *fuga mundi* (fleeing from the world) but also of *odium mundi* (hating the world). The thick walls and iron bars and grates were there to serve as a necessary separation from that world in order to protect the monk or nun from the vices and evils of the world. Further, for women, the cloister served not only for safety or to grow in virtue but also to protect their virginity. Thus, full claustration was considered paramount for religious women: dying to self, permanent reclusion, absence from public view, total silence, being unseen and unheard.

Clare's vision of the cloister was quite different, contrary even. For Clare it would be more properly called an enclosure, and her approach to it would be more fluid, as she would seek to define for herself what it meant to her. For Clare, the enclosure—though fully embraced—was not the cardinal feature of her vocation; it was ancillary. Clearly, Clare emphasized the evangelical life being lived fully therein. For Clare's calling was not to retreat from the world, but rather to evangelize and witness. She was the woman of light—"a city set on a hill cannot be hidden" (Mt 5:14).[84]

In this, the enclosure for Clare could never be a closed wall to keep others out; instead, she was "open." In something of a paradox, for Clare, reclusion would mean openness. Instead of a wall, the enclosure for her was more like a ring to protect and nurture her spirituality and that of the women who would follow her. In this, they could evangelize without. Clare would one day write, "For the Lord Himself has placed us as a model, as an example and mirror not only for others, but also for our sisters whom the Lord has called to our way of life as well, that they in turn might be a mirror and example to those living in the world."[85]

The only time Clare wrote about the enclosure, she said, "May you cling to His most sweet mother who gave birth to a Son Whom the heavens could not contain, and yet she carried Him in the little cloister of her holy womb and held Him on her virginal lap . . . so you, too, by following in her footprints especially those of humility and poverty, can, without any doubt, always carry Him spiritually in your chaste and virginal body."[86]

Here, the enclosure is not a physical place, it is a personal space. It is not an edifice of stone walls, but it dwells interiorly within the body and soul—the womb—of every sister (or every believer). The enclosure is the most personal and intimate place where, by imitating Mary in humility and poverty, we welcome and embrace the Lord. In this, the enclosure for Clare was alive: it breathed, prayed and sang, rejoiced and praised God.

Thus, Clare's future life within the enclosure of San Damiano would be distinct from the ancient form of religious life, and she would allow for more flexibility in her practice of it. In fact, while the monastic tradition prohibited cloistered sisters from leaving the monastic walls unless seeking to establish another monastery, Clare, instead, would permit a sister to go outside of the enclosure if she had a "useful, reasonable, evident, and justifiable purpose." This was a significant departure from the religious form of life for women and reflected the influences at work in the Church and society of her day.[87]

As Francis rebuilt the *outside* of San Damiano with rocks and mortar, Clare and her sisters would be living stones on the *inside*. There, she too would respond to the Lord's command to rebuild. What Francis constructed with his hands, she would build with spirit. Clare would be as a living cloister who, with her sisters, prayers, and presence, would edify the church interiorly and spiritually. And together their efforts would go far beyond that little church, reaching the heights of the universal Catholic Church.

In sum, Clare's form of life at San Damiano would encompass a twofold calling: enclosure and openness. Inside the enclosure, she would seek to *safeguard* the spirituality and form of life—especially regarding poverty—that she had received from God through Francis. And this she would *begin* to transmit to others: first to those who would join her in her life, then to those who would come to her for direction, and finally to the greater Church at large. True to its namesake, many would be healed at San Damiano.

Ultimately, Clare's form of life within the enclosure of San Damiano would be simple: "To observe the holy Gospel of our Lord Jesus Christ, by living in obedience, without anything of one's own, and in chastity." This was the life Clare chose, and this is what she sought with all her heart.[88]

> *Her mind was not completely at peace [in San Angelo in Panzo], so that, at the advice of Saint Francis, she moved to San Damiano.*
>
> LEGEND 4:10

10

JUST ONE PRIVILEGE

For lo, the winter is past, the rain is over and gone. The flowers appear on the earth, the time of singing has come, and the voice of the turtledove is heard in our land.

Song of Solomon 2:11–12

ONCE they passed through the gate of San Damiano, Francis showed Clare and her sister around. There, she felt a deep peace and a profound joy. In the silence and stillness of the little church and cloister, she felt holiness envelope her in love and security. For there in that little space were no privileges except one: poverty.

Clare sensed that this was the ideal place for her to follow in the footsteps of the lesser Christ—the first and truest minor. She knew immediately that it fully exemplified the charism that Francis, and now she, sought so wholeheartedly to follow.

For Francis, poverty was the primary charism he had received from the Lord, and it underpinned everything else he did. For Clare, it would be no different: the bedrock of her new life had to be built with poverty at its foundation. There, she would fully and radically embrace poverty; it would be the heart of her life.[89]

First, the location of San Damiano was ideal. It was well outside the city walls of Assisi. The town walls for the people in Francis's and Clare's day did more than just protect the city from invaders: they delineated the boundaries of identity and belonging. Within the walls were so many districts and neighborhoods that, despite the civil war fought just a few years earlier, were still separated by class and status.

But around San Damiano, instead, were the marginalized and the poor: the sick, the thieves, and the lepers. And this is where Clare, too, would live—with the outcast. By living outside the walls, Clare would be outside the social context of Assisi as well as the city's politics and social practices. And she would be free of it. Like Francis, Clare, too, would live poor among the poor. In this, not only would she have solidarity with them, she would become like them.

Further exemplifying poverty to Clare was San Damiano's function. In addition to serving the local farmers and poor people, it was also used as a place of refuge for pilgrims—known as Romeos—passing through the Spoleto Valley on their way to or from Rome, as it was located just off the old road known as the Via Antiqua.[90] And it was busy, as the old road was an important and well-traveled thoroughfare connecting Perugia and Foligno. Further, just beyond Perugia to the west ran the important medieval road, the Sienese Via Francigena, that conjoined Rome with France, whereas to the east of Assisi—through Foligno—ran the ancient Roman road, the Via Flaminia, that conjoined Rome with the Adriatic Sea.

Clare thought for a moment about the pilgrims who passed through San Damiano. She, too, would live like them: poor and dependent on Providence. She, too, would like to live as a "pilgrim and stranger," like the prophets of old who had no earthly country of their own, but belonged only to a heavenly one.[91]

To the right of the church were some simple huts and small rooms. Francis told Clare that when he began coming to San Damiano just after his conversion, an old priest named Father Peter lived there.[92] Behind the dormitory was the sacristy where he vested for Mass. Francis, too, had stayed with him in those rooms in the early days of his conversion while he was in hiding from his father.

"When I stayed here with Father Peter, he called these rooms the *Domus Presbiterale* (priest's house); however, one day these rooms will be a *domus fratrum* (house of friars)." Francis looked at Clare and Agnes and smiled.[93]

Francis then accompanied the two sisters inside the church and kneeled down. Clare, too, kneeled with Francis. And there she saw it for the first time: the Byzantine crucifix. She had heard the story countless times. This crucifix, still hanging in the church's nave, spoke to Francis, giving him his life mission: "Francis, go and rebuild my house, which, as you can see, is totally in ruin."

Francis then led the pair past the crucifix through the door to the right of the altar. They walked down several stone steps to a low area that wrapped around the rear of the altar. Clare looked around and then closed her eyes imagining it all. This would be the space for her prayer choir. There would be plain stalls made of undecorated wooden panels with equally simple wooden hinged benches for standing or praying. With just two simple reading lecterns, the barren stone floor, the little window facing east to let in just enough light, it would the ideal place for prayer.[94]

There the sisters would pray the Liturgy of the Hours together, simply and without chant. *If a sister did not know Latin*, Clare thought to herself, *she would be taught. Or she could pray Our Fathers corresponding to the Psalms*. In any case, there would be no privilege given to sisters from noble, literate backgrounds.[95]

Francis and Clare then went behind the church to an exterior building jutting out to the left. There were two large rooms with plain walls. These rooms once provided shelter for the pilgrims. In the first room was a long rough wooden table with benches and a simple wooden crucifix on the wall. Clare thought to herself that this room would be the refectory. *In the next room*, she thought, *the sisters would sleep*. There would be no cells or beds, and all the women would sleep together on mats directly on the floor in that one large room.[96]

Then Francis led Clare and her sister outside. On the south side of the church was a beautiful patch of land with a spectacular view of the valley. As she looked around at the land, Clare thought that the amount of space was ideal. The amount of land within the fence was not very spacious. But it had to remain that way; there could be only enough for a little garden. She and the sisters would eat simply what they could grow. *Here we will have a simple garden that we will work with our own hands. This will provide for our sustenance*, Clare thought to herself.[97]

The way of life Clare envisaged could not encompass vast expanses of land. For land ownership evoked feudalism, still in practice. Being the daughter of an upper-class land-owning family, Clare was all too familiar with the realities inherent with land possession. She grew up seeing how her father and uncles employed the less fortunate servile class to toil the land and thus profit from it. And all too often that land had to be defended with thick walls, tribunals, and sometimes even arms.

In Clare's brief stay at the Benedictine monastery of San Paolo, she saw how religious communities, too, utilized land as a source of income. When noble women entered, they brought dowries of land and possessions with them; in fact, for the *choristae*, dowries were a requirement for entrance. Through rents, tithes, and fees for usage, monasteries and abbeys used land to sustain themselves economically and maintain self-sufficiency. Over time, however, many had acquired such vast expanses of land holdings that the abbots and abbesses were elevated to the aristocracy—a privilege they did not mind. No, Clare did not want large tracts of land. San Damiano would boast no such privileges or security.[98]

Therefore, when women came, she could not accept land dowries or property endowments from them. For dowries not only increased the wealth of the monastery, they also created special privileges for the noblewomen who entered. While in San Paolo, Clare had also observed how the dowries of wealthy choir nuns led to a privileged way of life within. But San Damiano would be different: there would be no distinction between highborn and lowborn women. All would be sisters and equal.

Here, Clare thought, *there will be no rank or titles. Instead, we will all be sisters in genuine community. There will be no privileges or distinctions between choristae or conversae. In this, the community will live together as a family of sisters in community, belonging, and intimacy.*

And neither will there be an abbess, Clare thought. At San Damiano, Clare would lead the other sisters primarily as a servant. She could not rule over them as a powerful abbess. Instead, she would seek to be as a contemplative mother, even a sister, to the women. In this, Clare believed that her leadership would be modeled after the words found in the Gospel of Matthew: "Whoever would be first among you must be your slave; even as the Son of man came not to be served but to serve, and to give his life as a ransom for many" (Mt 20:27–28).[99]

The only requirement for entrance would be to give away whatever she owned—if she owned anything. Any woman who would enter San Damiano would have to do what Francis did and what she did. They, too, would have to pose the same question to the Lord as the rich young man who inquired how to inherit eternal life. And, if they wished to live in San Damiano, they would have to do the same: "Go, sell what you have, give the money to the poor, and come and follow me."[100]

But there were questions that had always been on Clare's mind since she began considering following Francis. How would she and the sisters be provided for? How would she be able to meet the needs of the community? How would she reconcile embracing poverty within the very real limitations of the enclosure? The brothers were not cloistered, and they had the freedom to go out and beg alms. Clare and the sisters, however, did not.

Clare knew in her heart that the answer lay in Providence. She had faith with all her heart that God had called her there and would surely provide for her needs. But how? In a practical sense, Clare believed the friars would help them.[101] Further, Clare believed that if she sought to help the laypeople spiritually—through prayer, spiritual counsel, and presence—they would, in turn, give back to the sisters materially. Certainly there were many generous and pious laypeople who would bring flour, oil, wine, and other foodstuffs for their sustenance.

However, Clare was also wise enough to know that they would not always be able to rely on others to provide for their needs. The sisters would surely need more than the few meager rations of table vegetables they could grow or that were brought to them. She and the sisters would have to work. Though she was of noble status, Clare's mother had taught her the value of working with her hands, and Clare knew how to spin. She was a seamstress and would sew while the other women who would come could utilize whatever talents they had.

Clare thought about how the Monastery of San Paolo was structured. There, the highborn nuns did no manual labor, which was considered work for the lowborn lay sisters. Clare, however—in another departure from the way most women's monasteries functioned in her day—would eliminate that practice: in San Damiano, all the sisters in the community would work equally. It would not matter if they were highborn or lowborn in the world; in San Damiano, they would share the burdens equally. Thus, the work roles would have to be rotated, especially the most humbling ones, which Clare herself would do.[102]

However, Clare believed that their work should be a service, not a business. Therefore, she determined that there should be no fixed prices on her work. Instead, she would give away the fruits of her labor, accepting only alms or gift offerings in return.

Francis and the two women then returned to the church and knelt before the crucifix of San Damiano. He prayed the prayer he had once made there in front of that same crucifix: "Most High glorious God, enlighten the darkness of my heart and give me, Lord, a correct faith, a certain hope, a perfect charity, sense and knowledge, so that I may carry out your holy and true command. Amen."[103] They asked the Lord to show them the way and to do his will always.

Francis then saluted his two sisters and left the church. As he passed through the gate, he closed it and went back into the world. Clare, however, remained inside with her sister.

Clare was overjoyed at her new life. However, despite her enthusiasm, she had doubts. Would the life she envisioned at San Damiano prove too difficult for other women? Would they come? Clare pondered these things in her heart as her first day in San Damiano came to an end and darkness enveloped the land.

After praying with Agnes, Clare lay down to retire for the night. After she drifted off to sleep, she had a dream. It was vivid, colorful, and extraordinarily realistic. Francis appeared to her holding a mirror. He handed it to her and told her to look into it. Then he disappeared.

Clare looked into the mirror. Instead of seeing a reflection of herself, however, she saw her mother. Ortulana was gazing back at Clare with a peaceful demeanor. Then Clare saw her father standing next to her mother with his hand on her shoulder. He, too, appeared serene. Next, she saw her sisters, aunts, and the women of her neighborhood of San Rufino. Next to the women were uncles and cousins. Behind her immediate family members, Clare then saw her grandparents, who had been deceased for some time, and then their parents and theirs.

Clare then saw the priest who had baptized her as an infant and administered the other sacraments to her. Next to him, the bishop of Assisi, Guido, appeared holding a reliquary with some relics of San Rufino, the patron saint of Assisi. Then Clare saw the poor of Assisi—the marginalized and sick she had served. Then some of Francis's friars appeared, including her cousin Rufino and Philip.

In that dream, Clare saw every person she had known in her life, all those who had accompanied her in her life. And then, suddenly, they vanished. Then Clare saw only a reflection of herself with the crucifix of San Damiano behind her.

Francis then appeared to Clare again in the dream and told her to turn the mirror over. She did so and looked into the other side of the mirror. This time, she saw the face of her sister, Agnes, with her religious veil covering her head. Then other women began appearing. Next, there was Pacifica, and then some other women she had known from childhood or from the district of San Rufino. Clare's other sister, Beatrice, appeared, as did her own mother, Ortulana. Clare was struck that they were all wearing a veil.

Then women from all walks of life appeared in the mirror, too. They were from the upper nobility as well as poor commoners. Many were from Assisi or nearby towns and cities, and Clare recognized them. But then women from beyond Assisi—whom Clare did not know—began appearing, too. Clare saw dozens, then hundreds of women from cities and villages all over Italy. Then they were in the thousands. They came from beyond the Alps—from all nations—and they spoke all languages.

Clare saw that they were all wearing the same veil and tunic. And they were all kneeling before the crucifix of San Damiano. Finally, they all disappeared, and once again Clare saw only the reflection of herself.

Francis then came to her again, took the mirror from her, and blessed her. And Clare woke from her sleep.[104]

She looked over at her sister, Agnes, who was still sleeping. A deep peace came over her as she thought of all those people she had known in her life. She gave thanks to God for who she was now because of each one of them.

Then Clare looked around at the empty dormitory of San Damiano. She had no doubts: they would come . . . Yes, they would come. She rose and went into the chapel to praise God. She thanked God again for the great mission he had given her and prayed for strength to carry it out.

There [in San Damiano], as if casting the anchor of her soul in a secure site, she no longer wavered due to further changes of place, nor did she hesitate because of its smallness, nor did she fear its isolation. This is that church for whose repair Francis sweated with remarkable energy and to whose priest he offered money for its restoration. This is the place where, while Francis was praying, the voice spoke to him from the wood of the cross: "Francis, go repair my house, which, as you see, is totally destroyed." In this little house of penance, the virgin Clare enclosed herself for love of her heavenly spouse. Here she imprisoned her body . . . here on a path of penance she trampled upon the earth of her members, sowed the seeds of perfect justice, and showed her footprints to her followers by her own manner of walking.

LEGEND 5:10

11

COMMUNITY

The maidens saw her and called her happy; the queens and concubines also, and they praised her.

SONG OF SOLOMON 6:9

THE next day, in fact, while Clare and Agnes were planting seeds in their garden, the third woman came to San Damiano. It was one of Clare's closest confidants, Pacifica. She was the woman who had accompanied Clare's mother on pilgrimages. And she was also the woman who had accompanied Clare to her meetings with Francis as well as the on night of her departure to St. Mary of the Angels when she left her father's home.

Then something unusual began to happen. A new spirit began taking hold of many of the young women of Assisi and surrounding cities and towns. Families talked about it over supper; women gossiped about it at the cisterns and market; men discussed it at the fairs and mills; the city's *podestà* and consuls were confounded. Even the priests and canons shook their heads in disbelief at what was happening. What started as a trickle soon became a great flood as more and more noblewomen left their well-to-do palaces and chose, instead, the poverty of San Damiano. The castles and fortresses of the nobility were being emptied of the most promising young women!

Next came Benvenuta from Perugia. Clare had known her as a girl when her family took refuge in her father's house in Perugia while in exile during the civil war of Assisi. And then there was Filippa, the daughter of Leonardo of Gislerio. Her father, like Clare's, was a Major nobleman of Assisi, and his castle, too, had been destroyed during the civil war.

Ginevra came next. She was the noble daughter of Giorgio, the son of Ugone. She entered San Damiano and changed her name to Benedetta (Blessed). She would indeed be blessed among the women of San Damiano as she would succeed Clare as abbess after her death and would be tasked with the building of the great basilica of Clare to honor her and safeguard her remains.[105]

And then came Cristiana, the daughter of Bernardo of Suppo, who had lived within Clare's house during her childhood. And then Agnes, the daughter of Oportolo, joined. The daughter of Lady Diambra, Balvina—who left her father's castle in Valfabbrica—came, too. And then there was Massariola, the daughter of Lord Capitanio. A second Cristiana came, too; she was the daughter of Lord Cristiano, a consul of Assisi known for his wisdom and learning. Then came Grazia and Completa, who changed their names to Illuminata and Agata. Both daughters of Tomassino, the lord of Monteverde, came as well. Other sisters, Matilde and Agnina, came and changed their names to Iacopa and Chiarastella.[106]

These women were erudite and cultured, and they read Latin and the classics. They played instruments and knew how to dance. They wore fine gowns and jewels. All would have made most pleasing brides for a fortunate bridegroom. But they had other desires.

They had spent their girlhoods listening to the knightly tales of chivalry and courtliness. They, too, had dreamed of being swept away by a great prince. Their imaginations had run wild as they dreamed of the lord who would steal their hearts. They had sought to make themselves more desirous by embracing the virtues of prudence, silence, modesty, and humility. But in the end, the One who eventually came for them was not just any lord or prince; he was the Lord of lords, the Prince of princes.

Like Clare, these noblewomen had been world-weary. They knew what it was like to live surrounded by those striving for ever more money, land, security, and feuds. Many of them, like Clare, had experienced the plight of uprisings and civil war firsthand and had felt the sting of loss. Some, like Clare, knew what exile and marginalization felt like. But all of them longed for another way.

And they found that way through the sermons of Francis and the friars. That flame within their souls was ignited as they, too, longed for a different Spirit. Not the spirit of the present age, but the Spirit of the Everlasting Age. When they listened to Francis preach, they felt a joy they had never experienced in this world, because it came from the Other World. What they discerned in the life of Francis and Clare was a foretaste of true peace—that peace of which Christ spoke when he said, "Peace I leave with you; my peace I give to you; not as the world gives do I give to you" (Jn 14:27). And the small flame grew into a fire.

Thus, they, too, interrogated their Christ and asked him what they needed to do in order to gain eternal life. Like the rich young man and so many faithful followers of Christ, they, too, had kept the commandments: they had not killed, committed adultery, stolen, or borne false witness. They had honored their parents and loved their neighbor as themselves.

Yet they believed there had to be something more than merely being good, and they longed for the perfection Christ called some to in the Gospel. It was that perfection Christ offered to those when he said, "If you wish to be perfect, then go, sell what you have, give the money to the poor, and come and follow me." But, unlike the rich young man, they answered yes. And they did it joyfully.

Thus, they gave away or sold whatever they owned and renounced what was theirs to inherit. And they arrived in San Damiano not with dowries, titles, or property endowments but only with the noble clothes they were wearing. And these noble vestments they promptly exchanged for the most noble of vestments: the undyed penitential tunic and the veil.

But not all who came were wealthy noblewomen; girls from the class of commoners came as well. And they were not all from Assisi either, as they came from the nearby cities of Spoleto, Trevi, Montefalco, Foligno, Spello, Bevagna, and as far as the Tiber Valley.

And then one day, someone nonchalantly opened the door to the church. It was a day like any other. While Clare and the other sisters were busy at work in the common room, two more women came unannounced. When one of the sisters discovered them kneeling in the church, she rushed up to tell Clare and the others who was there. They could not believe the news. They stopped what they were doing and raced down to the church. They were amazed at who they saw.

There, in prayer before the crucifix of San Damiano, was Clare's own mother, Ortulana. The woman who had been Clare's teacher now kneeled before her and placed herself under the obedience of her own daughter. It would now be Clare who would be mother and teacher to Ortulana. Together with Ortulana was her youngest daughter, Beatrice. Now all three sisters and daughters were reunited with their mother in San Damiano. That day was never forgotten by the women of San Damiano.[107]

In all, some fifty women followed Clare in San Damiano. The names of the community of sisters are tenderly conserved on a parchment penned by a notary in 1238. It remains to this day attached to an ancient wooden lectern in the choir of San Damiano.

They are introduced as "Disciples of Saint Clare in San Damiano," and their names are listed in Latin in three columns: Clara (Abbess), Agnes, Philippa, Jacopa, Illuminata, Cecilia, Aegidia, Agnes, Anastasia, Agnes, Christiana, Jacopina, Balevina, Mansueta, Amata, Benevenuta, Bonaventura, Benevenuta, Benerecevuta, Consolata, Andreas, Aurea, Leonarda, Agata, Felicitas, Angeluccia, Felicitas, Massariola, Maria, Gregoria, Maria, Joanna, Benedicta, Joanna, Bennata, Joanna, Lucia, Elias, Mattias, Clara, Stella, Lea, Beatrix, Bartholomea, Praxedes, Erminia, Daniella, Clarella, Pacifica, Vertera, and Patricia.

The parchment is authenticated at the bottom, "*Ex rogito notarili Perusiae A.D. 1238 n. XIV.*"[108] Curiously missing is the name of Clare's mother; there is only a bold, enigmatic note at the bottom of the parchment stating, "*Absens Hortulana, S.ctae Clarae Mater*" (Absent is Ortulana, the Mother of St. Clare). Was she away for a "useful, reasonable, evident, and justifiable purpose"? Or had she perhaps already passed from this world?

It is clear that Clare loved all these women not just as abbess but as a mother. It is also equally evident how much these women loved Clare. Indeed, when the sisters testified about Clare, they spoke of a woman who lived a life of extraordinary, even heroic, virtue.

During testimony at Clare's canonization process, Sister Pacifica said that Clare was always humble, kind, and loving to all the sisters. When she ordered a sister to do something, Clare always wished to do what she had commanded. And if any were sick, she had compassion on them and served them by washing their feet and mattresses.[109]

Sister Benvenuta, too, said that Clare was always very humble and that she carried out the most degrading chores personally, even cleaning the toilets of the sick sisters with her own hands.[110] Sister Filippa said Clare always served others in the community, gave them water, and covered the sisters at night when it was cold.[111] Sister Amata said that Clare had countless graces and virtues and further noted that she displayed the highest virginity, kindness, meekness, and compassion toward all her sisters.[112]

Sister Cristiana said that Clare's holiness and habits of virtue were so great that it was impossible to even speak of them; if she could have compared her to anyone else, it would have been to the Virgin Mary herself.[113] Sister Cecilia said that when Clare emerged from prayer, her face appeared brighter than usual and there would be a certain sweetness around her mouth.[114] Sister Balvina said that Clare was diligent and solicitous in prayer, contemplation, and the exhortation of her sisters. She was humble and wore harsh clothing; she slept on a bed like a table and kept stringent practices of fasting and abstinence.[115]

In the beginning, after the initial community had formed, Francis returned to see the sisters. And it was then when he saw that the life Clare had envisioned the day she arrived in San Damiano was indeed fulfilled. From within the enclosure of San Damiano, Clare and the sisters embraced the aspects of the new life wholeheartedly: poverty, minority, and community.

Francis examined Clare and the other sisters and saw that they did not shirk from deprivation, poverty, or hard work. He rejoiced and was moved as he looked at all of them. He marveled at what God had done and gave thanks to him for having fulfilled the prophecy. And he was grateful that each woman had responded to God's call.[116]

He then gave them a new name: "Poor Ladies." In the nobility of the poverty they had chosen, they were ladies and dames, for they had chosen the highest and most gallant way. They were now wed celestially to the highest Lord, the greatest Prince.[117]

Francis then made a promise that would remain dear to Clare's heart and that she would never forget. He promised that he would continue to accompany them always and that he would have the same care and concern for them as for his brothers: "Because of divine inspiration you have made yourselves daughters and handmaids of the most High, most Exalted King, the heavenly Father, and have taken the Holy Spirit as your spouse, choosing to live according to the perfection of the holy Gospel. I resolve and promise for myself and for my brothers always to have the same loving care and special solicitude for you as for them."[118]

Clare then turned to Francis and promised him obedience, "I, together with my sister, have ever been solicitous to safeguard the holy poverty which we have promised the Lord God and you, blessed Francis. So, too, any sisters who shall follow and succeed me here are also bound inviolably to observe it to the end, that is, by not receiving or having possessions or ownership of any kind."[119]

Francis, true to his word, assigned some friars to live in San Damiano to assist the sisters. Their names were Bentivenga, Marco, and Gilio.[120] They lived in the priestly residence to the right of the church, which was aptly renamed Domus Fratrum. There in the church, they served the sisters sacramentally and pastorally.

Yes, Clare was jubilant at the new community that was forming within. And the sisters within San Damiano rejoiced at being able to live with such a saint. Her light and fame had spread and people all over began to hear about her. Scripture was fulfilled: "You are the light of the world. A city set on a hill cannot be hidden" (Mt 5:14).

But not everyone was as enthusiastic as they were. In fact, while those within were rejoicing at their new life at San Damiano, some—outside San Damiano—already had plans to change it.

For within a short time the reputation of the holiness of the virgin Clare had spread through the neighboring areas and from all sides women ran after the fragrance of her ointments. Virgins ran after her example to serve Christ as they were; married women to live a chaste life more completely; nobles and illustrious women, spurning their ample palaces, built strict monasteries for themselves and considered it a great glory to live for Christ in sackcloth and ashes.

Legend 6:10

12

THE STRUGGLE FOR SAN DAMIANO

The watchmen found me, as they went about in the city; they beat me, they wounded me, they took away my mantle, those watchmen of the walls.

SONG OF SOLOMON 5:7

"BENEDICTINE?! Why would he impose the Benedictine Rule on us here at San Damiano? I am a little plant of Francis!" exclaimed Clare, bewildered.

The year was 1218 and Clare was in the speaking parlor at San Damiano. Her vicaress, Sister Benedetta, was seated next to her. She was reacting to the disconcerting news that Brother Philip, seated on the other side of the grille, had just brought.

Brother Philip was close to Clare and played an important role in her life; he had done so, in fact, since even before she entered San Damiano.[121] He was mediating between Clare and Cardinal Hugolino of Ostia who had appointed him as the first visitor of San Damiano. It was no easy task. He was the bearer of bad news.

The cardinal was charged by Pope Honorius with incorporating a number of expanding women's communities into the Church. He was seeking a change of direction in

Clare's community, as well as a number of other women's communities in central Italy. Many (including the Dominicans and Cistercians) had been neglected by their mendicant male counterparts who were unwilling or unable to accept the stability required to guide them. Therefore, in an effort to guide them toward stability and security, Hugolino decided to place them all under the Benedictine Rule.[122]

Making matters more difficult for her was the fact that her sister Agnes had been sent to Monticelli, near Florence. She was sent to found and lead a new monastery following the form of life of Clare. Clare was feeling heartache over the separation. And now she had to bear this new cross.[123]

"I have spoken personally to the cardinal," began Brother Philip. "I already told him that you will not be pleased to live under the Benedictine Rule. He believes, however, that it is in your best interest . . . as well as that of the Church." Clare listened intently. She tapped her finger fretfully on the wooden bench she was seated on.

"He is concerned about many things," Brother Philip said to Clare. "He worries about the stability and security of your way of life. He is concerned about other women's monasteries as well. As you know, many other communities are seeking to emulate your life here at San Damiano, and the cardinal is troubled for their safety and well-being, too." He paused for a moment as Clare listened carefully.

"There are also other questions, too. But the primary issue is his concern that your community, based as it is on poverty, may not be self-sufficient. The reality is that he has serious doubts that your community will remain viable over the course of time."

"Viable?!" Clare shot back. "I hold the cardinal in the highest esteem; in fact, he was here with us as a guest in San Damiano not long ago.[124] Yet, are not the words of Our Lord and Savior himself viable enough? He who said, 'If you would be perfect, go, sell what you possess and give to the poor, and you will have treasure in heaven; and come, follow me'; 'Take nothing for your journey'; and 'If any man would come after me, let him deny himself and take up his cross daily and follow me.'" Clare was citing the scriptural passages that led Bernard of Quintavalle to give away his possessions and become Francis's first follower. These words were the scriptural basis that formed the foundation of the life of all followers of Francis, including Clare and the women.

"I did not leave the wealth, prestige, and security of my father's house for the stability and treasures of a religious monastery!" Clare exclaimed. "I want not to 'store up treasures on earth'; instead, it is my wish to 'store up treasure in heaven, where neither moth nor decay destroys, nor thieves break in and steal.'"

Clare was concerned that if the community of San Damiano were forced to accept the Rule of Benedict, their community would settle into another monastic foundation. Her way of life had to be Franciscan—based on poverty—not Benedictine or monastic.

"I understand and I agree with you," responded Philip. "All the brothers do, especially Francis. But the cardinal sees it differently. He is partial to the Benedictine Rule, as it is eight centuries old and time-tested."[125]

Clare continued, "But poverty is the foundation of our way of life. Like you and the brothers, we, too, wish to live as mendicants, albeit within the confines of this cloister. I realize that poverty creates instability and insecurity in this world. However, that is precisely what necessitates us to seek stability and security in the Lord! We wish to embrace the same radical poverty as you and Francis. We wish to appropriate nothing to ourselves; instead, we wish to place all our 'hope in the Lord.'"

Clare continued to protest to Brother Philip, though he was on her side. "We must not become monastic! We have chosen a poor life here in San Damiano outside the city walls. We desire to be like the poor and marginalized people near us. We prefer to serve them, not the other way around."

She continued as if seeking to convince Brother Philip, "We have always refused to accept dowries here. When I took refuge at the Benedictine convent of San Paolo of the Abbesses, I observed the distinction between the noble-born *choristae* and lowborn *conversae*. The nuns from noble backgrounds are served by lowborn nuns. Here at San Damiano, we have completely eliminated any such distinction by requiring that every woman give away whatever she owns—if anything at all—before entering. Here no one enjoys a privileged status and we are all equal." Clare motioned to Sister Benedetta seated to her side to indicate how she was dressed identically to her.[126]

"We all serve one another," Clare continued. "To encourage mutuality in community, we have a weekly chapter meeting when everyone—including myself—confesses her faults. I also consult with every sister regarding any issue involving the whole community."[127] Brother Philip did not speak a word, and he just listened.

Clare was pensive for a moment and then continued, "But even though we will not accept money or possessions, nonetheless we work. You must tell the cardinal that we are not idle. Our days are full with prayer and work. Together we pray the canonical Hours. We also have time for private and personal devotion. Then, when not praying, we not only sow and spin, but we are constantly cleaning. I also look after the needs of the community. We have enough land for a vegetable garden, which the sisters and I tend to in order to grow our own food. We also perform manual chores and assignments that are rotated on a monthly basis."

Clare then paused as she thought about the implications of a Benedictine Rule. Sister Benedetta was troubled, too.

"I have only respect for the Benedictines," she continued after a few moments. "The good women of San Paolo put themselves at great risk by accepting me in their monastery after I left my father's house."

She paused as she shook her head, "But I fear that a Benedictine Rule will make us into something we are not. The monastic tradition involves possession and ownership. It employs rents, dowries, businesses, titles, and the strict enclosure. It is founded on stability." She paused again.

"Here we have avoided the trappings typical of the traditional monastic *stabilitas*," she persisted. "Instead, we get by through donations or offerings in exchange for services. We also have the friars and extern sisters who help us meet our needs.

"Has the cardinal perhaps taken issue with my practice of the enclosure?" Clare asked, although she did not wait for a response, as the question was merely rhetorical.[128]

"At San Damiano, we do observe the cloister, but to the degree that it aids the spiritual life. For us, the enclosure is sacred space that enables us to nurture an intimate relationship with Jesus. Inside the sacredness of the enclosure, we are free to focus on the enclosure of the heart. The walls serve to create an environment within which we can cherish, protect, and enhance our sense of intimacy and spirituality." Brother Philip continued to sit silently and patiently listen.

"But we do not believe that the enclosure should be a barrier to shut out God's greater plans. As such, I allow the cloistered sisters—with special permission—to go outside the convent for useful and reasonable purposes. Also, when we are in serious need, I do permit the extern sisters to go outside the enclosure to beg alms."[129]

"The cardinal understands," replied Philip finally. "However, Hugolino also feels the need to ensure your safety, as he is concerned for your protection. Even some of the friars have concerns about the location of San Damiano out here. You are well outside the city walls and there are many who do not believe it is safe for you." Now Clare and her vicaress listened.

Philip continued. "From the point of view of Cardinal Hugolino and other prelates, their focus is first and foremost on safeguarding your security. They want assurances for your safety as well as your self-sufficiency. And they feel that a Benedictine Rule is the best way to guarantee both."

Clare just sighed as she whispered to herself, "But the Lord is faithful; he will strengthen you and guard you from all evil."

Brother Philip then changed directions. "Clare, you should know something else. You are up against more than just a cardinal. There is also a decree of the Lateran Council, which forbade the establishment of new religious rules."

The Fourth Lateran Council had just taken place in 1215. It was a watershed event in the Church, in which, among other things, Pope Innocent III sought to curb the growth of poverty movements. In an effort to avoid confusion and make sense out of the many new spiritual movements (some orthodox, some heterodox), it was declared that any new movement must be steered into one of the existing rules.[130]

"You know very well that the Council declared that any new religious movement must assume one of the existing rules—either Benedictine or Augustinian," continued Brother Philip. "Francis received oral approval for his form of life in 1209 by Pope Innocent III *before* the council. Therefore, our way of life was exempt from the regulation."

Clare was certainly aware of the Fourth Lateran Council and its effects on the new religious and lay movements that were springing up in the Church throughout Europe. She also knew of the skepticism that some within the hierarchy felt toward the new mendicant movements based on poverty. Now that such communities were attracting women, they were even more skeptical.

Clare responded forcefully, "But just two years ago, Pope Innocent III orally approved our request to not own property. And that was *after* the Council."[131] She then thought for a moment and added, "Plus, it was Francis himself who gave us our form of life based on poverty in 1212. Since we received his guidance as well as that of

Innocent's permission before the council, should that not exempt us from its decree?"[132]

Clare did not give Philip a chance to respond before posing the next question with grave concern, "Could it be revoked? Could our privilege of poverty be revoked?" There were things that Clare was willing to mitigate, but her stance on poverty was resolute.

"Will he force us to own property or possessions?" she asked again, enunciating each word slowly.[133]

Brother Philip shook his head, saying, "I do not know." He, too, was concerned, and he repeated, "I do not know, Clare . . . I do not know.

"You are not alone, Clare," he finally added. "The women who follow Brother Dominic of Guzman are in the same position. And so are the Cistercian sisters." He hoped that a sense of solidarity would help her feel better. Brother Philip really did feel compassion for Clare and their plight. Clare took notice.

Clare now sought to reassure Philip. "Well, then, the lord cardinal must know that we profess strict obedience to the Church," she said. "We are not associated with the teachings of Joachim of Fiore or Amaury of Bène.[134] Nor do we wish to follow in the footsteps of the likes of Valdès of Lyons, the Albigensians, or the Humiliati.[135] We are simply followers of Francis walking in the footsteps of our Lord, Jesus Christ, in Gospel poverty. It is my utmost desire to remain part of and be obedient to the Holy Father and the Church. In no way do I want my community to be outside the authority of the Holy Father. For I believe wholeheartedly that the will of God is mediated through the Church—the Holy Roman Church."[136]

"Clare," replied Philip, "the good cardinal knows that you are orthodox in your beliefs and obedient in your way of life. He certainly acknowledges that. However, the upshot is that the cardinal does not believe that women can live as you are living . . . at least for very long." Clare sighed.

"Look, Clare," Philip continued. "Even if you can remain self-sufficient here in San Damiano, you must also understand the effect your community is having on other women's communities. You know how important women's monasteries are in civic affairs, not just religious. Therefore, this is not just a question between San Damiano and the cardinal; it is an issue between you and countless city councils and municipalities throughout Italy, and even beyond the Alps. The *podestàs* and consuls are furious at what is happening."

In the Middle Ages, it was common for women to enter monasteries for reasons other than religion. Some were widows or could not marry; some were orphans or illegitimate daughters; others had birth defects or health problems. Therefore, it was in the interest of the city authorities—in addition to the Church hierarchy—to ensure that women's monasteries functioned smoothly.

Clare listened patiently as Philip told her what she already knew. "Countless women's monasteries are embracing your way of life, Clare. Monasteries for women all over are switching to a form of life modeled after your community here in San Damiano. Many of these communities are not recognized by any authority—either civil or religious. And many women are entering these communities against their families' wishes. You know all this . . . Therefore, it is important to both ecclesial leaders and ordinary citizens alike that this community of San Damiano functions smoothly.

"The rule of life the cardinal is seeking for you here in San Damiano will have implications elsewhere, as your community here is the protomonastery for all the communities seeking to live your way of life. What happens to San Damiano will affect all the communities." Clare sat back and shook her head.

"I understand," she said after a moment. "I should have sensed a Benedictine Rule coming after I was forced to accept the title of abbess.[137] I never liked that title, as it implies to me monasticism and hierarchy," she said with a sigh. She sat there for a moment, tapping her fingers uneasily. Sister Benedetta noticed and tenderly took Clare's hand to reassure her. Clare acknowledged her and smiled.

Philip nodded in agreement. "He's behaving how a good *paterfamilias*—a good head of a household—would act toward his daughters. That's all." He now reached through the iron grille and touched her hand to console her.

He then told Clare what he believed she should do. "Clare, your challenges are threefold: you must remain faithful to the charism of poverty that God has given you through Francis; you must be obedient to the ecclesiastical prelates who have authority over you; and you should be sensitive to the reality of the social and ecclesial period in which we are living, especially as it pertains to women. I shall pray that our generous Lord reveals to you the way to reconcile these three concerns."

Finally, Philip paused as he prepared himself to break the last piece of difficult news he had for Clare that morning. "Clare, there is one last thing . . . ," he said hesitantly. Now it was Brother Philip who was tapping his finger apprehensively. Clare took notice.

"There is also the difficulty of . . . how shall we say . . . pastoral assistance." As he said this, he spoke with heartfelt sincerity.

"We both know that Francis himself promised you that he would always assist you and the community here in San Damiano always . . ." Philip looked directly into Clare's eyes trying to gauge her response. But she remained steady. He continued.

"You should know, first of all, that we all give thanks to God for the tremendous growth that has taken place here and in the other women's communities." Philip paused and looked at Clare again. This time, he could discern her unease growing.

He spoke in fragmented phrases as he searched sensitively for the appropriate words. "However, as friars, we are discovering . . . we are learning . . . that it is proving rather . . . er . . . let's say challenging . . . to meet the needs of the women's communities. You are expanding so much.

"The demands . . . the strains on our resources have proved . . . rather extraordinary . . . We often struggle to find the alms to meet our own needs . . . And now there is the additional effort of trying to provide for you . . . and the other women." Clare's heart sunk as she understood what he was about to tell her.

"Well, Clare . . . Know that we are doing what we can. Francis loves you very much . . . and all of the sisters . . . as we all do, too." As Philip said this, his voice cracked and he struggled to hold back a tear. It was painful for him to have to explain to Clare what he knew was in store for her in the future.

He composed himself as he concluded, "It's just that . . . Well, things are different now . . . We're all growing and things are changing . . . And we just don't have the resources we once did."

"We understand, Brother Philip," Clare reassured him. She reached over and took the hand of her sister seated next to her.

"The good Lord is with us and will never abandon us. We are sure of it," Clare said as she tried to mask the unease that was growing inside of her.

"Well, then, we will pray for your consolation during this period. You can be assured of that, Clare," said Philip as he prepared himself to leave.

"Thank you, Brother Philip," she replied. "And please communicate to the good cardinal all I have told you," she said, returning to the previous discourse. Clare was confident the Lord had led her to poverty and would not abandon her. She would accept nothing other than full permission to live poverty.

"You must make it abundantly clear that we want nothing here other than one privilege: that of poverty. Please tell the cardinal that we will in no way acquiesce to anything other than one form of life: that of following Our Lord in radical minority and total poverty. Hugolino is close to Francis, and I know he will be fair and just." Clare spoke with full composure, though her heart was pained.

"Yes, we can be sure of that," replied Philip. With that, the three stood up, and Philip blessed Clare and Benedetta. He then left San Damiano. As he walked back down to St.

Mary of the Angels in the valley, he thought about how Clare's desire to possess only poverty seemed bizarre to those in the world. She seemed to exemplify the words of Scripture from St. Paul: "For the word of the cross is folly to those who are perishing, but to us who are being saved it is the power of God" (1 Cor 1:18).

Clare went directly to the oratory where she kneeled down and began to pray. Her heart was hurt, and a strong sense of unease was growing within. She trusted in the Lord with all her heart, but she also knew all too well how frequently God put his loved ones to the test. Would she have the strength to endure what lay ahead?

In the year 1218, Cardinal Hugolino did indeed require the community of San Damiano to accept the rule that he personally wrote. It was Benedictine. Based on social, practical, religious, and juridical considerations, he was acting to find a balance between Clare's way of life and her charism of poverty for women with the context of the times they were living in. Thus, he sought to steer Clare's nascent Franciscan movement for women toward a more stable way of life with a focus on security, autonomy, and stability. His way of life for them was, in effect, more monastic.[138]

However, he respected Clare's utmost desire, and he did not require her community to own property, even if the exemption was limited, canonically, to her community of San Damiano.

The following years were particularly difficult and painful for Clare, as she felt misunderstood, even forsaken, by many within the Church. But the biggest feeling of abandonment was yet to come. The man who had promised to always be there and accompany her was changing, too.

Pope Gregory of happy memory [formerly Cardinal Hugolino], a man as very worthy of the papal throne as he was venerable in his deeds, loved this holy woman intensely with a fatherly affection. When he was [attempting to] persuade her that, because of the events of the times and the dangers of the world, she should consent to have some possessions which he himself willingly offered, she resisted with a very strong spirit and would in no way acquiesce. To this the Pope replied: "If you fear for your vow, We absolve you from it." "Holy Father," she said, "I will never in any way wish to be absolved from the following of Christ."

LEGEND 9:14

13

THE *TRANSITUS* OF FRANCIS

My beloved had turned and gone. . . . I sought him, but found him not; I called him, but he gave no answer.

SONG OF SOLOMON 5:6

EVERYONE knew how fond Clare was of Francis. To Clare, he was her "blessed father," and she often referred to him as her "founder, planter, and helper."[139] It was Francis who had been her "pillar of strength, her one consolation, and support."[140] She often dreamed about him, including once when Francis appeared to her and nursed her with spiritual nourishment.[141]

It was Francis who had inspired Clare the most since the beginning of her conversion. It was Francis who had given her enthusiasm for the new way to live the Christian life. It was Francis who had stirred her to embrace poverty. It was Francis who had moved within her the radical decision to leave home and follow him with nothing. It was Francis who had led her and instructed her.

Indeed, when she arrived in San Damiano, Francis promised to always have the same care and concern for Clare and the sisters as he had for the brothers. And so it was. In the beginning, according to some of the early writers, Francis came to San Damiano often and met with

Clare and the sisters. They enjoyed frequent fellowship and community together. And he continued directing Clare and the other women.[142]

At times Francis even turned to Clare for counsel in making important decisions in his life. Once, in the early days, he was feeling tempted to give up preaching to dedicate his life to solely that of a hermit.[143] Not trusting in his own discernment, however, he asked another brother, Sylvester, as well as Clare and the holy sisters to pray for him to know the will of God. Clare and the sisters received the same response, as did Brother Sylvester: Francis was called by God, not only for himself, but to bear fruit and bring others to God. He had to continue preaching, they told him.

There was also the time when Clare left the confines of the enclosure of San Damiano and met with Francis and the brothers for a meal. For a long time, Clare had desired to meet with Francis and the brothers outside of San Damiano to break bread with them. And after much insistence, Francis finally consented. They met at St. Mary of the Angels, the place where Clare was tonsured and veiled. Accompanied by several brothers and another sister, Clare walked from San Damiano down to the church dedicated to Our Lady of the Angels. And there they set the table on the bare hallowed ground.

The friars and sisters spoke together of holy and spiritual things. In fact, it is said that a mysterious light emanated from where the communion of brothers and sisters were seated. It was so bright, in fact, that the sky lit up. The townspeople, believing that the church and friary of St. Mary of the Angels was actually burning, came in haste to put out the fire. Instead, they found Clare and Francis with a sister and the brothers seated around a table together completely enraptured. That day was never forgotten by Clare and the brothers.[144]

But now all that was in the past. At first Clare tried to deny it to herself. But it soon became increasingly clear and impossible to refute: something had changed in Francis. Clare noticed it when his visits to San Damiano became increasingly rare. And then, suddenly, he stopped coming altogether. After that, his brothers, too, did the same. They all stopped coming.[145]

Clare and the sisters were dismayed. Why had he and the other brothers pulled away? What happened to him? Clare was beginning to feel as if he were actually breaking his promise never to abandon them.

After much insistence, Clare was able to convince Francis to return to San Damiano to preach. The sisters were overjoyed to listen to his sweet voice once again, as it had been so long since they had heard his holy sermons. Francis's preaching was always so powerful, and whenever they heard him, they felt filled with the Spirit. So the sisters eagerly gathered in the choir stalls behind the crucifix in great anticipation of Francis's arrival. But none could have anticipated what was about to happen.[146]

When Francis arrived, he went straight to the crucifix and kneeled down. Instead of speaking, however, he remained fixed before the crucifix with his head bowed in complete silence.

After a few moments, he stood up and made a strange request: he asked for a cup of ashes to be brought to him. Clare readily complied. She went to the fireplace, scooped up some cinders, and placed them in a jar. Francis then sprinkled some ashes on his head and poured the rest around him, forming a circle. He then sat down on the floor in the center of the circle of ashes and remained silent for a long time.

Finally, he stood up, and it was clear he was about to speak. The sisters leaned forward in their choir stalls readying themselves to savor each of his words. However, instead of preaching a sermon, he repeated the first three words from Psalm 51 over and over: "*Miserere mei Deus . . . Miserere mei Deus . . . Miserere mei Deus*" (Have mercy on me, O God). Then he stood up and abruptly left. The sisters looked at one another baffled. Some even began to cry. Even Clare was left confounded.

During this period, Francis always had a cough and he often looked peaked, pale, or emaciated. He was in pain and constantly ill with one ailment or another. He ate little and slept even less. Only those closest to him knew what happened to him on the mountain of Laverna, that he received the marks of the crucifixion of Christ on his hands, feet, and side. Clare knew about it and had tried to ease his suffering by sewing him a pair of special slippers. Walking was particularly excruciating for him, as the stigmata were like nails protruding from his feet.[147]

Then one day in the spring of 1225, it seemed that Francis would return to them when he requested to come to San Damiano. Clare and the sisters were overjoyed that he would be staying just below their dormitory in the friars' residence next to the church. Yet even there, he found no remission of his suffering as he was tormented by not just his illnesses (he had picked up an eye disease in the Holy

Land and could not tolerate light) but also mice that disturbed him.[148]

To their sorrow, Francis kept to himself and spent fifty days there in prayer and solitude instead of engaging the sisters. In a corner in one of the rooms, he created a little hut by hanging mats from the ceiling. There, his eyes would not be disturbed by the light of the sun or fire. Yet still his silence continued.

Unbeknownst to Clare and the sisters, Francis was dictating a series of praises for the created world around him. Despite his suffering and the fact that he could barely see, he praised God for all the elements of creation. In what would come to be known as the "Canticle of Creatures," Francis gave thanks to the Lord for all his works—from Brother Sun to Sister Moon.[149] Yet he seemed oblivious to the women. And still his silence continued.

In a feeble effort to regain his health, Francis left Assisi and was brought to Rieti to undergo treatment. He was prescribed various herbal remedies or potions of crushed precious metals to drink. In an effort to recover his eyesight, doctors attempted the cauterization of his temples. All was for naught, however, and his ailments worsened.

Francis could hardly eat now, and his body began to seriously decline. His liver appeared infected, and his stomach and limbs began to swell. When he began vomiting blood, the doctors told him there was nothing else they could do. At that point, Francis requested to be brought back to Assisi. He wanted to spend his last day in the place he loved more than any other: St. Mary of the Angels.

When Francis returned and the people saw him, they began considering the impossible. No one would say it out loud, but everyone was thinking it: "Could this be the end?" It seemed inconceivable, as Francis had been so strong, so omnipresent. He was only forty-four years old. How would they fare without him? Even the friars, when speaking about Francis amongst themselves or to the sisters, spoke solemnly and in hushed tones. No one would dare say what they all seemed to know: Francis of Assisi was dying.

Clare knew it, too, for she could feel it in her heart. During this period, she longed to see him again just one last time. Even though she was ill herself, she wanted with her whole being to be with him, to console him, to sit with him in his final hours. But even though she requested his presence there at San Damiano, he did not come. This last request of hers was refused. And still his silence continued.

Though Clare had wholeheartedly and freely embraced the enclosure of San Damiano, it now began to truly seem like a prison: the thick wooden doors and bars, the iron grilles and grates felt like a burning incarceration. This, coupled with her own sickness, led her to feel trapped for the first time in her life. It was as if she were in a cell, not only in the cloister of San Damiano, but also in the pain of her own heart. She wanted just a last word with him, one final blessing, a farewell.

And still she could not understand: why the heartbreaking silence?[150]

Clare prayed for him constantly, as did all the sisters. They prayed for him during communal liturgy in the choir stalls, individually in the church before the crucifix, and in the oratory. Clare also went outside to the garden where she prayed. There she kept constant watch over St. Mary of the

Angels down in the valley—that place where Francis lived and the place where she received the tonsure.

Then one night in early October, as Clare lay down, she drifted off to sleep thinking about him and praying for him. She knew he was lying there surrounded by his brothers, dying. Suddenly, with a gasp, she sat up startled. Her heart was racing. She sensed something spiritual taking place. It was happening.

Though it was an unusually chilly night and she was not well, she arose and wrapped herself in her mantle to fend off the biting cold. She descended the tall stone steps from the oratory and went outside to the garden. She looked up at the sky. It was crisp and clear. The moon was full and vibrant and all the stars were out.

She looked down at St. Mary of the Angels in the valley; it was illuminated under the moonlight and stars. Something unusual was taking place: a great flock of larks was circling the sky above St. Mary of the Angels.[151] They were singing beautifully and joyfully, though it was the middle of the night. Then Clare knew. She fell down to her knees and wept there on the cool, moist grass. It was Sunday, October 4, the year 1226.[152]

There are few moments in the life of any of us that mark us as does the loss of a dear loved one. As Clare mourned the loss of her beloved Francis, who knows what took place within the heart and soul of that thirty-two-year-old saint? What did she think and feel? How did she respond? What did she do? Did she react stoically as a haloed saint up on a lofty pedestal? Or naturally as a person with very human sentiments and emotions? The sources only say that Clare was ill and that she and the other sisters wept profusely. As for the rest, it is pure conjecture.

When one of the friars reached San Damiano early the next morning with the official news, he was only confirming what Clare and the sisters already knew: Francis had breathed his last. And now he was gone, and she would never see him again in this world.

The young friar stood below the crucifix in the sanctuary and spoke to all the sisters who had gathered in the choir stalls to receive the word. Clare and her vicaress, Sister Benedetta, sat in front of them, behind the grate, closest to the friar.

He somberly recounted how it happened.[153] He said that Francis's last request was to be laid on the bare ground, stripped of all his garments, next to the Church of the Portiuncula. But Brother Elias, the acting minister general of the order, would not give his consent, and the brothers instead covered him with a wool blanket.

"Francis told us to never leave the Portiuncula, as he loved that place more than any other," the brother said softly. "He then told us to remain faithful to poverty and to the Catholic Church, and he gave the Gospel preeminence over any other rule of life. Francis then asked Brother Leo to read from the Gospel of John.

"Those were his final words," the young brother said. "And then he expired," he added. As he said this, he began weeping, as did Clare and all the sisters.

After a few moments, Clare wiped her eyes. With her head still down, she asked, "Who was there with him?"

The young friar said that Francis died surrounded by his closest companions: Leo, Angelo, Rufino, and Masseo.

And then, perhaps with a bit of naiveté, the young friar mentioned that Lady Jacoba of Settesoli was there, too. At the mention of her name, Clare looked up attentively. Sister Benedetta took notice.

Clare knew of Lady Jacoba. She and Francis were close friends. She was a Roman noblewoman from a wealthy family and had known Francis from the early years. Jacoba met him in 1209 when Francis was in Rome seeking papal approval for his life. Francis had given her spiritual direction, and she had joined the recently formed Third Order for laypersons. She was a great benefactress and had donated property to the brothers in Rome. In Trastevere near the Tiber Island, for example, she had given the friars some land they now used as a hospice for lepers.

"But Brother, how is it that she, Lady Jacoba, was there with Francis and the friars?" Clare queried the young friar. "Women are not permitted inside the enclosure of St. Mary of the Angels," she added with utmost seriousness. "Francis always strictly forbade any woman from ever entering the cloister. Surely he would not have allowed her to enter."

The friar then sought to enliven the mood somewhat. "Yes, you are right, Sister Clare," he said, now smiling for the first time since he arrived in San Damiano. "Francis never permitted women to enter the enclosure. However, this time he allowed for an exception, as everyone knows that Francis was fond of Lady Jacoba." As the friar spoke, the vicaress glanced over at Clare with concern. The young friar did not notice.

"Every time she visited him," he continued with a smirk, "she always brought her legendary almond pastries, which she personally baked for him. Francis loved them. They're quite tasty, I might add." The friar smiled as he spoke the last sentence. But he did not realize that he was the only one smiling.

He continued naively, "Yes, it is true that some of the friars protested, saying that no woman may enter the enclosure. But Francis made an exception saying, 'Well, let her be called, then, Brother Jacoba so that she may enter the enclosure and be with me and my brothers in my final hours.'" The young friar now beamed with satisfaction, proud as he was of Francis's cleverness.[154]

"We all know that Francis sometimes allowed an exception to the rules. And he wanted Lady . . . er . . . *Brother* Jacoba to be at his side in his final moments. And so it was." The inexperienced friar stood there smiling, expecting a lively response from the sisters. Instead, they remained stone-faced.

Clare suddenly arose and went up to the oratory where she knelt in prayer. "Why would he change the rule for her?" she wondered. "What about me?" she asked herself. She was the woman who had given everything away to follow him! And now she was here, imprisoned in a small country church outside of Assisi. Far from St. Mary of the Angels. Far away from Francis. All alone. And he was now dead. And she would never see him again.

Clare was feeling too weak to kneel, so she lay down there before the tabernacle. She reflected on her life. She thought about her adolescence when she was a little girl. She thought about her father, her uncle, her brothers, and cousins. She recalled how they dressed in full armor as they rode off on their destrier warhorses to do battle in jousts or other tournaments. They were so powerful, so robust. She had always felt safe and secure when they were around.

Clare then thought about the suitors—the men who had asked for her hand. There had been many. They were knights, too, and Clare could have lived as a true lady. She would have had castles, lands, and servants.

And then came Francis. How his sermons and words fired her imagination, she reminisced. He, too, seemed strong to her. But his was strength of a different sort. He was so mature and wise, so holy and spiritual. And she chose him! She gave it all away to follow him!

Now, for the first time, she began to consider that perhaps she had been wrong. She wondered if all this had been a mistake—youthful dreaming. Maybe God had never truly called her to this life—to religion, to poverty.

Some light I am to the world now, she thought to herself disparagingly.

Perhaps she should have listened to her relatives and remained in the secular world. She could have married and had children. Her sons would have been knights, her daughters ladies. She could have been like Lady Jacoba to Francis. She, too, would have been a great benefactress to him. She would have given him everything. She would have gladly donated her lands to him, and he could have built his hermitages. Her castles would have become his leper hospitals!

But instead, Clare was up there on the side of a lonely hill, locked away within the enclosure of San Damiano. And soon they would take Francis's body to a place somewhere within the city walls of Assisi, Clare ruminated. They would declare him a saint and do everything to keep his body safe and secure. Surely they would bury him deep underground somewhere for his protection. And she would never see him again.

Maybe she hadn't been good enough for him, she thought as she blamed herself for his silence. *Forgive me, Francis!* she shouted within herself. Clare wept profusely as she grieved and mourned, while the sisters let her be.

After a long time had gone by, Clare heard rustling and commotion below. At that moment, Sister Benedetta rushed into the oratory. "Clare, come quick!" She pulled Clare up by her arm. "You must come! Now!" she yelled as she practically dragged Clare down the stairs toward the choir.

Sister Benedetta rushed Clare past the stalls, which were empty. The heavy wooden door that separated the enclosure from the small nave of the church was half open. As Clare's vicaress pushed the door fully open, Clare could see the sisters standing in a circle below the crucifix in front of the altar. They were all weeping quietly. And there in the middle of the circle, underneath the crucifix, she could discern something . . . someone . . . lying on the floor.

When the sisters saw Clare, they opened the circle, allowing her to see and enter. There, lying lifeless on a litter on the stone floor of the church, was Francis.

Clare walked to him slowly. At first she couldn't believe he was there. She looked to her left toward the rear of the church. There she saw Francis's closest brothers: Leo, Angelo, and Masseo. Her cousin, Rufino, was there, too, as was Brother Elias. He was now the acting minister general of the order.

She stood there for a moment looking at them dazed. They returned Clare's gaze and smiled gently. Behind the friars stood a retinue of knights. They had brought Francis's body to Clare and the sisters.

Clare turned back to Francis. She kneeled at his side and took his hand in hers. Though it was cold, she took no notice. His eyes were closed, and he had a peaceful aura about him. She closed her eyes in prayer and sat there motionless with Francis.

Sister Benedetta went to the rear of the church and greeted Brother Elias quietly.[155]

"Before he died, he ordered me under holy obedience to bring him here," Elias said to her softly. Clare's vicaress looked at him gently.

"But it had to be after his death," he added. "He knew he caused her great suffering these last years." His voice crackled with emotion as he spoke.

"We, too, felt he was being too harsh on her, indeed all of you." Sister Benedetta listened without interjecting. Her eyes, too, glistened with emotion.

"This was something he wanted strongly . . . to come here," Elias said as he wiped away a tear. "Yesterday, as he lay there dying, he made me promise I would do it . . . I had to vow it," he uttered.

"The knights did not want to come here. They wanted to take his body straight to Assisi. They're going to inter him in the Church of San Giorgio for now, as it is inside the city walls. They're all afraid someone's going to come and steal his body, actually steal Father Francis's body!" Brother Elias said, forcing a smile.

"The Perugians, they're saying . . . It's the Perugians they say who are going to come and get him." He chuckled somewhat while Sister Benedetta smiled politely.

"Anyhow, I had to threaten to climb on top of Francis's body to force them to bring Francis here. And finally, they relented." Benedetta thanked him on behalf of Clare and the sisters.

"But he said it had to be *after* his death, not *before* . . ." Brother Elias continued with difficulty. "He wanted to come only after . . ." Elias trailed off as he swallowed hard.

"You know he loved her very much," he continued after a moment. "But he acted this way with Clare because he wanted to teach her . . . He always wanted to be her teacher . . . even if he had to be harsh." Elias now spoke intermittently between choking sobs.

"But we know . . . Of course you know, too . . . that he loved her very much." At this, he could no longer speak, and his body began to tremble. Sister Benedetta put her arm on his shoulder to console him.

"He lived only for poverty," Elias said finally after composing himself.

"He did what he did for poverty . . . all for poverty. And he wanted her . . . I think . . . to experience that fully. That is why he did what he did.

"I think she understands now," he added.

After a moment, Brother Elias reached into his tunic and pulled out a letter that he handed to the vicaress.

"He wrote this for her. I should have given it to her before, but we were not expecting him to go so quickly." Sister Benedetta took the letter and thanked him.

"He told me to tell her not to be sorrowful over not being able to see him," he told the vicaress. "He wanted her to know that she would see him soon enough."

Sister Benedetta glanced at the letter and smiled. She knew it would bring great consolation to Clare. As she put it in her pocket, she and Brother Elias looked over at Clare together.[156]

Clare opened her eyes and looked at Francis lying there before her. His eyes were closed, and his hands were folded one on top of the other over his chest with a small simple cross beneath them.[157]

His body was like a *Memento Mori*, Clare thought to herself as she gazed at him. For many centuries, monks and nuns kept human skulls or other bones in their cells as a "reminder of death." It was a way of remembering the mortality of the body and reflecting on the immortality of the soul. It helped them to focus their attention on the afterlife: heaven, hell, and the salvation of the soul. Some friars and sisters were using the practice of the *Memento Mori* as well.

As Clare looked at Francis's lifeless cadaver before her, she reflected on his life. In everything he did—his sermons, his direction, and all he had taught her—he always pointed to the cross. He sought to be "minor" in everything, to go down. He loved Jesus so much that he wanted to be with Jesus where he was: on the cross. For Francis, the cross was the greatest poverty. Clare placed her hands on top of Francis's hands and touched the cross underneath.

She then looked up at the great wooden Byzantine cross that presided commandingly over the small nave of San Damiano. It was that crucifix that revealed to Francis his lifelong message: rebuild God's house. It was at that moment when the cross impressed its signs on Francis's soul interiorly. Clare thought about how he spent the rest of his life responding to that command and to that cross. And, just two years earlier, it was that cross that had revealed itself on Francis's external body on the mountainside of Laverna when he received the stigmata.

Clare ran her fingers over the wounds on his hands. She kissed them. She then moved herself near his feet and touched them, too. She removed his slippers—the ones she had made for him—and kissed his wounds there, too. She then ran her fingers along his side and caressed Francis's wound underneath his tunic. She kissed his side through his tunic.

Francis truly lived the cross, she thought to herself, *which is the utmost and highest poverty.*

Suddenly, Clare realized something. Then, in that moment, everything made sense. She closed her eyes and began to tremble with emotion. At first she wept quietly, but the tears soon became a flood. They emerged from deep within. She now began sobbing profusely.

Everything she suffered those last years came out in that moment: her pain, loneliness, and suffering. The absence and silence of Francis, the misunderstanding on the part of the Church hierarchy, her loneliness there in San Damiano, her spiritual desolation. The sisters, still encircled around her, began to weep, too. So did the friars in the back. Even the knights were visibly moved, and some walked out of the church.

Eventually Clare became still. She now understood why he had been so silent those last few years, the meaning of the sermon of ashes. When the torrent of emotions passed, she opened her eyes and looked at Francis again. She looked at his face and moved closer to him. And now, for the first time in a long time, she smiled. Everyone was moved at the tender scene.

The young friar who had spoken earlier to Clare and the sisters watched Clare from the back of the church with the other friars. He now realized how imprudent he had been with her and the sisters earlier. Suddenly, in a moment of enlightenment, he knew he had something else to say to Clare. Sister Benedetta was still standing there with the brothers.

He walked over to her while Brother Elias moved so he could reach Benedetta. He said to her, "There is something I neglected to tell Clare earlier, Sister. There was one more thing Francis said before he died. I believe he would have wanted Clare to hear it, too."

"Please tell me," the vicaress said as she leaned closer to the young brother.

"Francis said to the brothers, 'I have done what is mine to do. Now may Christ teach you what is yours to do.' I know he would have wanted Clare to hear this as well." Brother Elias nodded.

Benedetta nodded as well. "Indeed, I believe he would have," she said as they both looked over at Clare.

She was still kneeling before Francis's body, but the tears were gone. Sister Benedetta noticed that Clare seemed different now. She was now joyful, and her face was once again radiating light. But it was a new, more vibrant light. Benedetta smiled, as she had feared that Clare's light had grown dim forever.

"Indeed, I have the strange sensation that she already knows what is hers to do," she said to the friar. "In fact, I think we all know what is ours to do," she added. Brother Elias nodded, as did the other friars. A warm consolation came over them all.

Francis was a teacher not only to Clare; both in life and now in death, he had been a teacher to all the sisters. And now they, too, understood more fully Francis's life, mission, and teaching.

Like Clare, they gave thanks to God for the gift of Francis and for his spiritual union. Indeed, they were now convinced more than ever that he had never abandoned them.[158]

After the *Transitus* of Francis, Clare understood her own vocation more fully. With her gaze fixed on the Lord, the graces, consolations, and spiritual gifts she had already received began to grow exponentially. Her consolation, strength, and support would now come from the highest Source. Though Francis had been her "founder and planter," it would now be God who would make her grow (see 1 Cor 3:6).

And she now knew what was hers to do. She would be true to her name, and her light would shine brilliantly. And for the rest of her days, she would seek to cast her light on one thing: poverty. For the rest of her life, Clare remained steadfast as one of his most devoted followers. Together with some of the early brothers who had known Francis, they formed an inner circle of Franciscans who remained as living testimonies to Francis and his dedication to poverty, a dedication and commitment they would have to safeguard with everything they had.

> *What else? By the most perfect poverty she was eager to conform to the Poor Crucified, so that nothing transitory would separate the lover from her Beloved or would impede her way with the Lord.*
>
> LEGEND 9:14

14

"GAZE, CONSIDER, CONTEMPLATE, AND IMITATE"

O that his left hand were under my head, and that his right hand embraced me!

SONG OF SOLOMON 2:6

THE days, months, and years of San Damiano were marked with the constant rhythm of prayer. Together the sisters prayed the canonical Hours—Lauds, Terce, Sext, None, Vespers, and Compline. They also listened to the Word read by the friars. Yet it was in personal prayer where Clare received many consolations and graces. It was then when she became most radiant and illuminated—the woman of "light."[159]

After Compline, when the sisters went to sleep, Clare often remained awake to pray.[160] Other times she would arise from sleep in the middle of the night to pray. She descended the steps from the oratory, passed by the choir, and pushed open the thick wooden door that separated the enclosure from the little church. There, veiled within the intimacy of the enclosure, she knelt in the nave underneath the crucifix.

This was her preferred time to pray—in the stillness of the night. While her sisters and the townspeople slumbered and all about her silence was at its fullest, she could hear the crucifix speaking. She spent countless hours over the years there in front of the crucifix of San Damiano praying, reflecting, meditating. For Christ's greatest teaching—the only theology Clare or the sisters ever needed—was fully expounded upon there in the cross.

The cross, in fact, represented the highest poverty to Clare, and she now turned to it with all her heart. Those who knew Clare were aware of the burning love she carried for the crucified Christ. She often cried over and poured out tears at his sacred wounds. She even taught the novices to weep over the crucified Christ.[161]

Clare often gazed up at the crucifix of San Damiano. And as she did, over a span of time, the Lord guided her. She received the words: Gaze (*intueri*); Consider (*considerare*); Contemplate (*contemplari*); Imitate (*imitare*). She reflected on these words and kept them close to her heart.[162]

As Clare remained in prayer observing the crucifix, she did more than simply look at it: she "gazed" upon it. Gazing for Clare was not simply "seeing" or "viewing"; when Clare gazed upon the cross, she opened all her senses, including mind and soul, and received a love story: that of God's love for humanity through Jesus's death, resurrection, ascension, and glory.

In the crucifix of San Damiano, the entirety of the passion and resurrection of Jesus Christ was illustrated. Jesus was crucified as a sacrificial victim, a Lamb, in remission for sins. Yet he had risen from the dead.

Though Christ was still nailed to the cross, he was not represented suffering as a *Christus Patiens*. Instead, he was standing upright, fully alive with his eyes open. His arms were wide open as an embrace of humanity and the Father. Christ has fully conquered death. The black background, a symbol of death, is dominated by an illuminated Jesus, who shows us life. "I am the light of the world; he who follows me will not walk in darkness, but will have the light of life" (Jn 8:12). Christ was resurrected and glorified. He was the *Christus Resurgens*. The scallop shells, outlining the icon, symbolize life: the mollusk dies, like the body, yet the shell lives forever, like the soul.

Several major figures stood below Jesus's outstretched arms: Mary, John, Magdalene, the mother of James, and the centurion. They were key witnesses to the event who received life from Christ's passion as droplets of his Precious Blood descended upon them. Smaller figures were present, too: Longinus (who pierced Christ with the sword) and Stephaton (the soldier who offered Jesus a sponge soaked in vinegar). Several angels observe the scene while a separate choir of angels above welcome Christ into heaven.

As Clare gazed on the cross, she *considered* its message of salvation. Here "consider" signified something to Clare much deeper than merely thinking about. Instead, Clare sought to "reflect," "meditate," or "ponder" the crucifix and what it meant. "Reflect upon," she once wrote, "the holy humility, at least the blessed poverty, the untold labors and punishments that He endured for the whole human race."[163]

When Clare "considered" the sacrifice Christ made on the cross, she realized how much God loved her, indeed, how much he loved all humanity. In his ransom, he revealed his humility and poverty. For it was the cross that taught Clare the highest poverty, as through it, Christ assumed the lowliest condition to connect with humanity. And he became poor in order that we would become rich.

By now Clare understood that poverty was about much more than land, material possessions, or money. For the Lord says in his Gospel, "Whoever of you does not renounce all that he has cannot be my disciple" (Lk 14:33). But now she understood the full meaning of the "possessions" Christ was speaking of. It was an emptying of all that did not come from God in order to embrace all that did come from God. True poverty, in effect, was in possessing nothing other than God and his love. And in total poverty, there was a wealth beyond measure indeed.

Clare later wrote, "If so great a Lord, then, on coming into the Virgin's womb, wanted to appear despised, needy, and poor in this world, so that people who were very poor and needy, suffering excessive hunger of heavenly nourishment, may become rich in Him by possessing the Kingdom of heaven, be very joyful and glad filled with a remarkable happiness and a spiritual joy."[164]

Clare now understood that the greatest and truest poverty was in living a life of complete and joyful surrender, just as Christ did on the cross. For in doing so, she fixed her heart not on the things of this world but on the things of the world to come. In completely surrendering everything, she had obtained the inestimable spiritual gift—the highest gift—that of accepting the will of God in all things.

As Clare spent more and more time in front of the cross, gazing and considering, she entered into another dimension. She began to *contemplate* the mysteries of Christ's passion and resurrection. For Clare, to "contemplate" was true to its etymology; it was like entering into God's temple.

There, in the silence of the enclosure of San Damiano, Clare closed her eyes as she meditated on the cross. Shrouded by her veil and removed from the world, she went deep down into the recesses of her mind and soul where there was nothing but sacred stillness and the fullness of God. Alone with the Lord, she pondered the deepest and most secret mysteries of the divine.

In contemplating the mystery of the cross and Christ's sacrifice, the Lord spoke to Clare, sweetly and kindly, within her heart. He told her many things, special things, and she received countless graces in those beautiful moments. God revealed to her truths about himself, herself, and the world around her. Many prayers were answered as God "whispered to her while others slumbered."

While Clare prayed and contemplated, she felt consoled and beloved. God was her Lord, her Lover, her most intimate Spouse. She knew she was desired "as a bride bedecked with her jewels" (see Is 61:10).

And soon her Lover revealed to her another mystery: she became aware that it was not she who was entering into God; rather, God was entering into her. Like Mary, another tabernacle, Clare, too, became aware of the awesome gift she had received: that of carrying the Lord within.

"Indeed, it is now clear that the soul of a faithful person, the most worthy of all creatures because of the grace of God, is greater than heaven itself," she once wrote in a letter to St. Agnes of Prague. "Since the heavens and the rest of creation cannot contain their Creator; only a faithful soul is His dwelling place and throne . . . As the Virgin of virgins carried [Him] materially, so you, too, by following in her footprints, especially [those] of humility and poverty, can, without any doubt, always carry Him spiritually in your chaste and virginal body holding Him by Whom you and all things are held together."[165]

In praying before the crucifix, Clare placed herself within the mystery of the incarnation, passion, and resurrection of the Lord. As the months became years while Clare remained there praying in her "temple of the Lord," slowly, as water running over a stone smooths it in time, something happened. She was changing. She was becoming like the God in whom she believed. She was transforming into God.

"Place your heart in the figure of the divine substance," she wrote to Agnes, "and through contemplation transform your entire being into the image of the Godhead itself, so that you too may feel what friends feel in tasting the hidden sweetness that, from the beginning, God Himself has reserved for His lovers."[166]

And this transformation Clare referred to was the ultimate outcome of her lifetime spent in deep prayer. It is also the ultimate outcome of the Christian life. In Christian theology, it is called "divinization" (*theosis* in Greek) and is the last of the three "ways" (or stages) referred to as the *Via Purgativa*, *Via Iluminativa*, and *Via Unitiva* (unity with God). For the Word became flesh not only to take away sin but also in order for us to "share in God's nature" (see 2 Pt 1:4). The Son of God became man so that we might become like him.[167]

And this was Clare's last word: *imitation*. Clare's desire to imitate Christ was not so much something that had arisen from her will; instead, it was a natural consequence resulting from the transformation that had taken place within her heart.

While contemplating before the crucifix, Clare often lost herself in spiritual rapture and ecstasy. Yet such delights never lasted long. For Clare soon heard the rustling of the sisters as they came down from the dormitory into the choir to pray community morning Lauds.

Now it is time to return to the community and the day's chores, she thought to herself as she arose and composed herself. Renouncing spiritual delights was never a sacrifice to Clare. For she was practical in her approach to spirituality. She was always concerned about the well-being of her sisters, the friars, and those outside the monastery who came to her. In fact, it was precisely her desire to imitate Christ that compelled her to go to others: the consolations she received in prayer were what she brought to them.

In this, Clare was a follower in the footsteps of Francis, who was also drawn toward others. Francis, too, spent time in prayer and contemplation up in the mountain hermitages. Yet he did so always to fill himself with God in order to return to the valley below, where he served the marginalized and preached.

However, both Francis and Clare were really walking in the path first trod by Christ. For it was Christ who alternated between praying in solitude and serving people. For though Christ often withdrew to the wilderness to pray, he was always called back down to the valley where he preached, healed, performed miracles, and taught.

Thus, Clare's imitation of Christ did not permit her to remain forever in contemplation, though she experienced God fully and sweetly there. Though her spirituality was indeed at times transcendent and otherworldly, she ultimately returned back into the world. In this, she was immanent and incarnational. Like Christ—the Minor who lowered himself, coming down from heaven to assume the lesser human condition of man—Clare, too, returned back to the "valley" of her cloister.

In Clare's Christian life, she wanted to be an example to the sisters and others. She wrote, "For the Lord himself has placed us not only as a form for others in being not only an example and mirror, but even for our sisters whom the Lord has called to our way of life as well, that they in turn might be a mirror and example to those living in the world."[168] For her example—her "mirror"—was Christ. And the light she received, she desired to reflect.

And when people heard about her "light," they came to her from all over. It was as if Clare had a third eye and could see things others could not. And Clare gave herself to them. She saw like God; she listened like God; she thought like God; she spoke like God; she acted like God. For she had a new hope and a new vision, one founded on Christ and his mysteries.

Clare's desire to imitate Christ led her to sacrifice herself entirely for her sisters and for all who came to her. And soon she would have the chance to make the ultimate one.

After the [sisters] went to their hard beds to rest their tired bodies, she remained in prayer, thoroughly vigilant and invincible, so that she could then secretly receive the divine whispers while sleep occupied the others.

LEGEND 13:19

15

SARACENS

Greater love has no man than this, that a man lay down his life for his friends.

John 15:13

GOD'S ways are oftentimes a mystery to us. Just when we think we know what the will of God is (or is not), God sometimes does the opposite and accomplishes the unexpected. "For my thoughts are not your thoughts, neither are your ways my ways, says the Lord" (Is 55:8).

In working out his will, God often accomplishes extraordinary things through ordinary people. Or, even more amazingly, he uses people of lowliness or meekness (and sometimes even brokenness) to do extraordinary things. And these things, in fact, would not be possible to those who are strong and great in the world. For "God chose what is foolish in the world to shame the wise, God chose what is weak in the world to shame the strong" (1 Cor 1:27).

Scripture is full of such people and events: the Hebrew people were generated through the incredible conception of an elderly wife; later, having been enslaved, an unlikely leader led them to freedom by performing miracles and confounding mighty Pharaoh; still later, a young shepherd boy brought down mighty Goliath to become king of

Israel. And, most amazingly, an angel announced to a poor Virgin that she would give birth to the Messiah, the Savior of humanity.

But the remarkable ways of God are not limited to biblical tales of long ago. Closer to home, Clare had just seen how God could use a broken man—still struggling in the aftermath of failed worldly ambitions—to rebuild his Church. And the young Assisian would be asked to do so equipped with nothing but poverty and the fervent conviction of his calling.

Now it was Clare's turn: she was about to be called upon to do her impossible task.

Perhaps it was asceticism and self-denial that had prepared her most for this day. Only the other sisters and those close to her knew of the harshness with which she treated her body. Instead of sleeping on comfortable straw mattresses, she slept on mats made of twigs or branches with a piece of wood as a pillow. She went without shoes and wore a rough pigskin garment or a hair shirt made of knotted horsehair underneath her rough tunic. She ate so little and fasted so rigorously that Francis himself and the bishop once had to order her to eat.[169] But perhaps it was precisely these penances that trained her to disregard her body and prepared her for what was to come.

Or maybe it was her altruistic service toward others. Clare was known throughout the land by now as a champion of the heroic virtues. She not only prayed for people's needs, she served them relentlessly and selflessly.

Surely it was all these things that had made her into the person she was. The poor, humble, crucified Christ had entered into her soul and transformed her into his likeness.

And she was now like him enough to do what she was called upon to do. She was willing to fully and completely "waste herself on Jesus" as that "precious oil" of Scripture.[170] Yes, she was ready for one of the defining moments of her life.

Clare and the sisters had been alerted that danger was imminent. The entire Italian peninsula was a volatile powder keg, as friction and discord were everywhere. City-states, municipalities, and republics fought amongst themselves for greater territories; Guelphs clashed with Ghibellines for power and control; lords brawled in the streets with each other or against commoners over feuds and grudges. One was either the aggressor or the defender as all jockeyed for power and control.

The foremost conflict, however, was between the emperor and the pope. The Holy Roman emperor, Frederick II, was agitated. The Hohenstaufen grievances with the German princes north of the Alps only made matters worse down on the peninsula, where the emperor struggled to solidify his empire. His kingdom—consisting of lands in northern Italy as well as the south, including Sicily—was being chipped away at by the myriad factions and strife. Yet it was the pope—that potentate of the Papal States in the center of Italy (and of his kingdom!)—that grieved him the most.[171]

Seeking a way out of the quagmire, Pope Gregory IX called for a council, but he was thwarted. Finally, the pontiff announced the excommunication of the emperor (the fourth time he had incurred that particular penalty in his lifetime) even referring to him as an Antichrist. The emperor responded by expelling the mendicant Franciscans and Dominicans from his northern empire and directing his troops against the towns and cities within the territories of the Papal States. It was all-out war against the pope.

To do his dirty work, Frederick used Saracens as mercenary soldiers. Out of fear of automatic excommunication, Christian soldiers would not serve under him. But communion with or expulsion from the Catholic Church was meaningless to the Saracens.[172]

On Frederick's orders, they would sack villages and towns allied with the papacy. The Spoleto Valley was a common target, as it was loyal papal territory. Caught innocently in the crossfire were the monasteries outside the city walls, which were, unfortunately, easy targets.

Particularly vulnerable were the women's monasteries. The wild brutes easily breached the walls and heavy gates and perpetrated the worst form of sacrilege by plundering and looting inside the cloisters. Sometimes they did atrocious things, unspeakable things, when they violated the nuns personally in the worst of ways. And that day, San Damiano was in their crosshairs.[173]

But those unsuspecting Saracens had no idea what they were getting themselves into. Unbeknownst to them, the women's monastery in their sights was headed by the daughter of a knight, the niece of castellans, the cousin of crusaders and cavaliers. Chivalry was in her genes. Courage, valor, and bravery coursed through her veins. They were in for the shock of their lives.

When they came, it was a Friday during the month of September, the year 1240. The hour was *tierce* (9:00 a.m.).[174] Suddenly, as if ghosts out of nowhere, they appeared "swarming like bees" at the walls of the monastery, frenzied and furious.

Clare had been sick for a long time, and she lay in bed in the dormitory above the church. When they came, the sisters were terrified. But Clare told them not to fear because the Lord would defend them. Raising her tear-filled face, she comforted the weeping sisters saying, "My dear sisters, I guarantee that you will not suffer any harm. You must have confidence in Christ."

Certainly, Clare had fear, too. The fact that she was courageous did not cause her to ignore what was objectively threatening and truly terrifying. However, her abiding faith in the actual presence of the Lord who is Emmanuel (God with us) gave her the strength to confront those fears, regardless of what might happen.

She then prostrated herself in prayer and, with tears in her eyes, cried out, "My Lord, do you wish to deliver your defenseless servants, whom you have nourished with your own love, into the hands of pagans? I beg you, Lord, defend these servants of yours who I am not able to defend at this time!"

Then, a wonderful and sweet voice—as that of a little child—was heard saying, "I will defend you always."[175]

"My Lord," Clare responded, "please protect this city, which by your love sustains us." And the Lord responded to her, "It will suffer afflictions, but will be defended by my protection."

In that moment, so many thoughts and memories flooded through her mind. She thought of her mother and how much she had sacrificed for her when she was a child. She thought of the abbess of San Paolo who had placed herself between her and her aggressors. She thought of Francis who had once gone to the Holy Land to offer himself as a martyr for peace.

But it was the supreme sacrifice made by the greatest Lord who made himself "minor" that influenced her most. She had spent a lifetime reflecting on the Crucifixion and what her Lord had done for her, indeed, for all humanity. She, too, yearned in her heart to imitate her crucified Lover. In fact, she had an ardent desire to offer herself, like Christ, as a sacrifice to save others. Like Francis, Clare, too, wished to be martyred. Perhaps this was her chance.[176] Clare knew exactly what she would do.

Taking to heart the words of Jesus, "Greater love has no man than this, that a man lay down his life for his friends," she said to her sisters, "I wish to be your ransom; if it should happen that the enemies come into the [monastery], place me before them."[177]

As she was unable to walk, she requested that the sisters and friars carry her down to the entrance of the refectory by the door to the courtyard.[178] She did not know what would happen to her, but her heart was filled with consolation as she thought of Christ being mocked, scourged, and crucified.

Like Christ, Clare, too, would surrender herself to her aggressors. But not without placing him between herself and them. Clare believed fully in the teaching of the Eucharist. She had often reflected on Francis's words when he spoke and preached on it. Francis often used to say, "I see nothing corporally of the Most High Son of God in this world except His Most holy Body and Blood."[179] When she received the sacrament of the Eucharist, she believed that the Lord she received hidden in the Sacrament was the same as him who ruled over heaven and earth. She was so devoted to the Eucharist that she regularly sowed corporals, the white linen cloth used during the celebration of the Eucharist, which she enclosed in silk or purple covers and sent to churches all over Italy.[180]

The Holy Eucharist was kept in a silver pyx inside an ivory box, as was custom then. She asked one of the friars to bring her the small box. And there, before the door to the refectory, Clare lay prostrate before her Lord, adoring him in the Eucharist. There she awaited what she believed would be her martyrdom. It was at that point when the Saracens broke through the gate and entered into the enclosure.[181]

During attacks, the hardened fighters were accustomed to one of two responses: people either fled in panic or they resisted with force. Instead, when the brutes rushed into the cloister, they were shocked at what they saw: a frail, elderly nun in a patched tunic lying prostrate before a mysterious box. Around her were other nuns doing the same.[182]

The Saracens stopped in their tracks, puzzled and confused. Instead of escaping or counterattacking, here was a powerless and vulnerable woman emanating peace and praying calmly before a strange box. She was not afraid of them. Her inexplicable vulnerability was disarming, her calm energy disturbing. Clearly this woman possessed a power not of this world.

And the Saracens were correct: Clare was indeed a citizen of a different kingdom. Their confusion was similar to that of Pilate who was troubled at Christ's answer during his interrogation: "My kingship is not of this world; if my kingship were of this world, my servants would fight, that

I might not be handed over to the Jews; but my kingship is not from the world" (Jn 18:36).

Clare, in her surrender to that kingdom, possessed strength infinitely more powerful than the soldiers with their weapons and physical force. She had received it by practicing the highest, most challenging imperative of the Gospel: "Love your enemies, do good to those who hate you, bless those who curse you, pray for those who abuse you. To him who strikes you on the cheek, offer the other also; and from him who takes away your cloak do not withhold your coat as well" (Lk 6:27–29).

In truth, Clare did not hate those who wanted to take her life and the lives of her sisters. Instead, she loved them and offered them herself as a sacrifice. In that moment, she possessed a peace the world could not give, peace that could come only from the Holy Spirit to a soul conformed to the humble, crucified, minor Christ of the Gospels.

For Clare understood the power and truth of the Gospel: that forgiveness and love defuse, that the highest bravery consists not in retaliation or self-defense but in sacrifice and dying to self, that true love has the power to transform self, society, and even adversary.

And, indeed, the Holy Spirit showed his might. The Saracens' confusion quickly turned to alarm as they began to fear something dreadful might happen to them. Their ferocity, rage, and excitement were transformed to fright. They promptly fled and left their swords, daggers, and shields behind. One can only hope that their surprise encounter with Clare (and the Gospel of Jesus Christ) initiated a conversion within their hearts.

On that day in Assisi, Clare witnessed not just to the Saracens but to all of us. She was a testimony to the power of one who prays and believes. She showed us what happens when one embraces the upside-down logic of the Beatitudes (see Mt 5:3–12). In a paradox possible only to those who had fully embraced the Gospel vocation of *minoritas*, what should have been a day of destruction and mayhem was divinely transformed into peace, grace, and holiness.

Clare's encounter with the Saracens showed the world what Jesus meant by assigning the "kingdom of heaven" to the "poor in spirit." Clare and the sisters were reminded how they were "daughters of God." In that moment, "they felt comforted," and "they saw the face of God." Everyone was shown mercy, including, in a special way, the Saracens themselves. Clare was a "peacemaker." And she was "blessed" indeed.[183]

> *The Spoleto Valley, more often drank of the chalice of wrath because of that scourge the Church had to endure in various parts of the world under Frederick, the Emperor. In it, there was a battle array of soldiers and Saracen archers swarming like bees at the imperial command to depopulate its villages and spoil its cities. Once, when the fury of the enemy pressed upon Assisi, a city dear to the Lord, and the army was already near its gates, the Saracens, the worst of people, who thirsted for the blood of Christians and attempted imprudently every outrage, rushed upon San Damiano, [entered] the confines of the place and even the enclosure of the Virgins. The hearts of the ladies melted with fear; their voices trembled with it, and they brought*

tears to their Mother. She, with an undaunted heart, ordered that she be brought, sick as she was, to the door and placed there before the enemy, while the silver pyx enclosed in ivory in which the Body of the Holy of Holies was most devotedly reserved, preceded her. . . . Without delay, the subdued boldness of those dogs began immediately to be alarmed. They were driven away by the power of the one who was praying, departing in haste over those walls, which they had scaled.

LEGEND 14:21–22

16

THE *TRANSITUS* OF CLARE

Awake, O north wind, and come, O south wind! Blow upon my garden, let its fragrance be wafted abroad.

SONG OF SOLOMON 4:16

IT was now 1253 and Clare was a sixty-year-old woman, elderly for that era. By now, she had been suffering from a prolonged sickness for some twenty-nine years. In 1224, the same year Francis received the stigmata, Clare began to suffer from mysterious illnesses. She could no longer walk and so rarely came down from the dormitory or oratory.[184]

Perhaps it was the harsh penances she had inflicted on her body that had taken their toll. Or maybe God had given her the unique grace of suffering together with him for the salvation of all. In any case, she believed that virtue was brought to perfection through illness, and she never complained. Instead, only words of holiness or thanksgiving emanated from her mouth.[185]

In addition to poor health, her struggles with the hierarchy continued unabated. Not only did Clare have to contend with her defense of poverty, she also struggled to maintain the presence of the friar chaplains in San Damiano.

In 1230, Pope Gregory IX had written a bull beginning with the words *Quo Elongati* that, among other things, prohibited friars from entering cloistered women's communities, including San Damiano. In typical fashion, Clare asserted herself, saying, "Well, then, let him now take away from us all the brothers [including those who beg alms] since he has taken away those who provide us with the food that is vital." Pope Gregory backed down and rescinded the prohibition.[186]

Despite her ailments and the countless tribulations she endured, however, Clare was at peace. As she looked back on her life, she gave thanks to God for the countless gifts she had received: her life and faith, her family, relatives, her sisters and the community of San Damiano. She praised God for her parents, who gave her life and baptized her in the Faith. She had no rancor or malice for any injuries received, but instead gave thanks for all in her life.

By now, Clare's reputation for holiness had spread well beyond Umbria, and she was highly regarded by the most eminent personages throughout Christendom with whom she is known to have corresponded.[187] Her biographer said, "The fame of her virtues . . . reached the palaces of duchesses, even the mansions of their queens. The highest of the nobility stooped to follow her footprints and left its race of proud blood for her holy humility. . . . Not a few, worthy of marriage to dukes and kings, did severe penance, and those who were married to rulers imitated Clare in their own way."[188]

Yet Clare also interacted with ordinary people who came to see her. By now Assisi was a pilgrimage destination. Since St. Mary of the Angels was honored with the plenary indulgence and Francis was sainted and buried within an ornate basilica, people from all walks of life stopped by San Damiano. They came to ask for prayers and healings, to have a word with her, or just to be in her presence. Though Clare's life was "veiled," she was open to all; people sensed something extraordinary within her. Through her intercession, they were all blessed and many were healed.

There was a little boy from Spoleto named Mattiolo whose mother brought him to San Damiano with a pebble lodged in his nose; by making the sign of the cross, the pebble was immediately expelled.[189] Another little boy who suffered from a prolonged fever was healed.[190] Again, with the sign of the cross, Clare healed yet another child who had a film over his eye. [191] And Clare healed still another boy suffering with fever and scrofula.[192]

Then there was a friar named Brother Stephen who suffered from a psychological disorder. As he frequently did with brothers or laypeople who needed strong intercessory prayer, Francis sent him to San Damiano to see Clare. After tracing the sign of the cross above his head, Clare allowed Stephen to sleep in the oratory where she usually prayed. After a short time, he arose refreshed and returned to Francis. He was completely healed from his insanity.[193]

But it was within her own community that Clare healed and worked the most miracles. Sister Pacifica, the first witness in the canonization process, testified that Clare healed five sisters merely by making the sign of the cross. There was Sister Benvenuta, who had been suffering for twelve years from a fistula under her arm that oozed puss. By making the sign of the cross, Clare healed her. She also restored Sister Amata to health from dropsy and a persistent cough, again by making the sign of the cross.[194]

Other graces and miracles took place within San Damiano as well. There was the time when the monastery's oil for cooking and anointing ran out. Clare called on Brother Bentevenga, who used to beg alms for them, to go out for oil. Before he came, however, she washed and blessed the jar. And when the friar arrived in San Damiano, it was already miraculously filled with oil.[195]

There was another miracle that the friars and sisters were referring to as the "multiplication of the bread." Once, an awful famine afflicted the town of Assisi, affecting the religious houses as well. The sisters' food was reduced to only half a loaf of bread. With complete confidence in Christ, Clare ordered Sister Cecilia to cut fifty slices from it. When she questioned her, Clare said confidently, "Do as I have told you." And when she did, miraculously there was enough bread to serve the entire community of fifty sisters.[196]

One of Clare's most legendary miracles, however, involved her supernatural ability to hear and see. One Christmas morning, Clare was too sick to go down to the choir for Morning Prayer. Though she desired fervently to be present for the liturgy in the choir below, she resigned herself to her illness and remained in bed. As she closed her eyes and began praying, however, she immediately saw and heard the entire Mass being celebrated by the brothers in the Church of St. Francis. She saw the entire liturgy in front of her and heard the chant of the friars and the musical instruments as if she were personally present. Due to this vision, in 1958, Pope Pius XII declared Clare the patron saint of television.[197]

Toward the end, Clare's reputation for holiness reached the highest summit of the Church: bishops, cardinals, and even popes corresponded with her and came to San Damiano to see her.[198] Cardinal Rainaldo, the sisters' protector, visited them often. Pope Gregory IX frequently sent Clare letters and correspondence asking for prayers and intercession for various people and needs; in July 1228, he visited Clare and the sisters while in Assisi for the canonization of St. Francis.[199]

Pope Innocent IV visited her on two occasions between the spring and summer of 1253. Once, upon hearing that she was ill, he hurried to see her from nearby Perugia with his retinue of cardinals. Clare later said that she felt blessed to have been visited by Christ twice that day: first, through Holy Communion administered earlier that morning by the provincial minister of the friars and, second, through the presence of his vicar on earth.[200]

On another occasion, a miracle took place when the pope came to San Damiano. Clare asked the Holy Father to bless some bread that had been placed on the table. Yet the pope deferred to her and requested that she bless it. After she objected, he ordered her under holy obedience to make the sign of the cross over the bread and to bless it in the name of God. And when she did so, a cross, clearly marked, appeared on each loaf of bread. Only some were eaten, while the rest were put aside to testify to the miracle.[201]

However, despite all the illustrious visitors, the graces and miracles that had taken place, and blessings in Clare's life, there was something still pressing on her heart. There was one thing left unresolved.

Clare had lived in San Damiano throughout five papacies: Innocent III (1198–1216), Honorius III (1216–1227), Gregory IX (1227–1241), Celestine IV (1241), and now Innocent IV (1243–1254). Each pope (with the exception of Pope Celestine, whose pontificate lasted only sixteen days) influenced her way of life, directly or indirectly, in various ways.

The Fourth Lateran Council of Pope Innocent III had the most lasting effect due to its prohibition against new religious orders. Seeking to execute its legislation, Pope Gregory IX (formerly Cardinal Hugolino) had the most direct impact on Clare's community through the rule he wrote for them as cardinal in addition to numerous proclamations and directives he formulated for Clare throughout his pontificate. (He also, unsuccessfully, tried to persuade Clare to own possessions.) Later, Pope Honorius sought to direct San Damiano in the form of various directives.

Finally, Pope Innocent IV, too, penned numerous directives aimed at the sisters. Yet it was the new rule he wrote for them in 1247 that affected them the most. In his rule, though he omitted references to "Benedictine," he added considerably to Hugolino's Rule. In fact, Pope Innocent not only imposed his new rule on San Damiano, he even ordered the sisters to accept it under holy obedience and not seek to be exempted from its form of life. Most distressing to Clare, however, was its obligation for them to maintain possessions for the good of the community. This newest rule was a direct threat to the privilege of poverty that was at the center of her life.

Yet even though the rules, directives, missives, and guidance provided by the pontiffs and cardinals rarely embodied or expressed the uniqueness of her vision of life, Clare always acted with obedience to the ecclesial authorities to whom she was subject.[202] However, the popes and cardinals had never truly understood Clare or the form of life she was seeking to live with all her heart. The form of life they were seeking to impose on her was based on required canonical norms and legislation or on other considerations.

And so Clare made up her mind. For, in truth, obedience does not mean passivity or powerlessness. She would set out to do something inconceivable. And her final act would, perhaps, be the most remarkable thing she ever accomplished. And she did it even though she had not studied theology and was ignorant of the unique Code of Canon Law that governed the Church and its orders. She did it even though she had never studied the liberal arts and was not exceedingly learned. She did it even though she was a humble abbess of a small country church. And she did it even though she was not a man.

She would write her own rule, her own form of life.

When she had finished it, her Rule—the Rule of Clare—would be the treasure of the whole of her life. For it would contain what was at the heart of the community of San Damiano. In it, she expressed and defined the form of life she had been called to by God through Francis. The Rule would seek to safeguard and cement the fullness of her Franciscan heritage and the one privilege she sought: poverty.

The Rule was summarized in the first sentence: "The Form of Life of the Order of the Poor Sisters that Blessed Francis established is this: to observe the holy Gospel of our Lord Jesus Christ, by living in obedience, without anything of one's own, and in chastity."[203]

The rest of the Rule consisted of twelve sections that were the culmination of her lifetime of prayer, penance, service, and leading the community in San Damiano. It dealt with accepting novices, prayer and fasting, responsibilities of the abbess, silence and the grille, working, the correction of sisters, the enclosure, and pastoral visitations. The most important part, however, dealt with her main charism, the thing that drove her, inspired her, motivated her, and which she sought her entire life: the privilege of poverty.

But it still had to be approved. And she wanted its approval to come from the highest cathedra of the Catholic Church: that of the bishop of Rome. But this was the same chair from which were issued countless guidelines not in alignment with her vision. Therefore, all Clare and the sisters could do was pray. But there was not much time left, as Clare was becoming ever sicker.

In the end, Clare was confined to her bed in the corner of the dormitory.[204] For her last seventeen days, she was unable to take any food at all. Despite her lack of physical nourishment, she nonetheless comforted and consoled all those who came to see her and became distraught at her state.

In her final days, she was rejoined by her earthly sister and the first woman to follow her, Agnes. She had returned to Assisi from Monticelli, near Florence, where she had served as abbess for twenty years. Like Clare, she, too, was advanced in age and was not well.[205] Some of Francis's early companions—Juniper, Angelo, and Leo—were with her, as well as a number of bishops and prelates.

After the doctors examined her, they said there was nothing they could do. Cardinal Rainaldo—bishop of Ostia, protector of the order, and friend of the sisters—was there. He gave her the last sacraments.

Finally, on August 9, 1253, Clare received what was the most beautiful gift of her life.[206] She was told that one of the friars had come with something important. As he came through the doorway from the oratory and approached her bed where she lay in the corner of the dormitory, Clare followed him with her eyes. With a gentle smile on his face, the friar handed Clare a leather parchment. As it was impossible for her to read, she motioned for him to read it. The friar unrolled the parchment and showed it to her. It was a papal bull.

He started reading the document, which began with the Latin words *Solet Annuere* (Let it be known).

"Let it be known. S. [Sinibaldus Fieschi].[207] For reasons known to me and the Procurator of the monastery, let it be known . . ." The friar was visibly moved. He paused and looked at Clare. She indicated for him to continue.

"Innocent, Bishop, Servant of the servants of God, to his beloved daughters in Christ, Clare, Abbess, and the other sisters of the monastery of San Damiano in Assisi, health and apostolic blessing . . ." He looked up again and began to smile as he realized what it was about to say.

He continued with emotion in his voice, "The Apostolic See is accustomed to accede to the pious requests and to be favorably disposed to grant the praiseworthy desires of its petitioners. Therefore, We have before Us your humble request that *We confirm* by Our Apostolic authority *the form of life that blessed Francis gave you and which you have humbly requested . . .*"

At this, quiet whispers of exultation and elation rose up among the sisters and friars huddled together around Clare in the dormitory. Agnes burst out sobbing, as she was overjoyed at the hoped-for news. The friar read the entire papal bull in which the pontiff accepted unconditionally the Rule that Clare had written. It had the full weight of papal authority. Clare, with tears in her eyes, smiled broadly.

What prompted the pope's change of heart will remain forever a mystery. Only the pope himself knew why he changed his mind and dispensed Clare from his earlier Rule. In any case, Pope Innocent IV had now granted Clare's final wish on her deathbed: the Rule she had written was confirmed by the highest authority of the Catholic Church. This was a remarkable feat, as it was the first time in the history of the Catholic Church that a woman had written a rule that received papal approval.[208]

Now her heart finally rejoiced. Clare could, like St. Paul, boast that she had "fought the good fight, finished the race, and kept the faith" (see 2 Tm 4:7). For the next two days, she kept that document close to her. She kissed it countless times and wept over it.[209] She was in total peace. She could go now. It was time.

Her final day in this world was two days later, August 11, 1253. It was the day after the feast of St. Lawrence, the deacon martyr, and the same day of the feast of Assisi's patron, San Rufino.

It was evening and night had fallen. Her final request was for the sisters to read aloud from the Gospel of John narrating the passion of the Lord. This was the same request Francis had made twenty-seven years before as he lay dying down in the valley at the Portiuncula.

Then, speaking to herself, Clare said, "Go without anxiety, for you have a good escort for your journey." She turned her eyes toward the door, which she gazed upon peacefully.

"Go," she continued, "for he who created you has made you holy. And, always protecting you as a mother her child, he has loved you with a tender love. May you be blessed, O Lord, you who have created my soul."

One of the sisters, Anastasia, confused as to whom Clare was speaking, asked her who she was addressing. The saint responded, "I am speaking to my own soul." In fact, Clare could see her soul's Escort who was standing not far away.

Then Clare turned to another sister, Benvenuta of Assisi, and asked, "Do you see, O child, the King of glory whom I see?" In that moment, Sister Benvenuta received a superabundant amount of grace and her vision, too, was illuminated. She looked toward the door where she, too, beheld the same heavenly vision.[210]

Sister Benvenuta later described what she saw: a multitude of virgins entered clothed in white garments; all wore gold garlands on their heads. One, more splendid than the rest, was walking among them. And on her head was a crown, which had at the top what appeared like an interlaced thurible. Instead of incense emitting from that censer, there was light. And the light was so splendid that it turned the night within the room into daylight.

The celestial virgin walked toward Clare and embraced her tenderly. The other virgins then brought forth an extraordinarily beautiful mantle with which they covered her. They decorated her bridal bed. Then, with a blissful smile, Clare's soul left her earthly body and passed on to the next world. Her *Transitus* was complete. Her light went out. She was gone. Her sisters were distraught at her departure, and they all wept.

> *Blessed is that passing from the valley of misery that became for her the entrance to a blessed life. Now in place of the farewell meal she is rejoicing at the table of the heavenly citizens; now in place of the coarseness of ashes she is decorated with a robe of eternal glory and is blessed in the heavenly kingdom.*
>
> Legend 29:44–46

EPILOGUE: LIGHT SHINES AGAIN—FROM SAN DAMIANO TO SAN GIORGIO

I am the light of the world; he who follows me will not walk in darkness, but will have the light of life.

JOHN 8:12

NEWS of Clare's death spread immediately, and a huge crowd went from the city down to the poor Church of San Damiano.[211] The *podestà* came with the city consuls. Knights arrived with their ladies. The canons from San Rufino came with priests from the various parishes. Merchants and artisans took a break from their work and came. And lowly peasants arrived with their poor children. Cardinals and other prelates came, too, with their jewels and rings to touch to her body, which was already considered a relic of powerful intercession. All were there to pay homage to the woman they believed was a saint and to witness her light one more time.

The next day, August 12, the Holy Father, Pope Innocent IV, returned from Perugia with his papal Curia. He was prepared to celebrate her funeral Mass directly from the liturgy of the Office of Virgins, for he was already convinced of her sanctity. The cardinal protector, Rainaldo, however, advised celebrating from the Mass of the Dead. It would be better to be prudent, he said, and wait for the canonization process to be completed. The pope acquiesced.

After the funeral Mass, it was decided to move Clare's body straightaway inside the city gates of Assisi. San Damiano was too vulnerable to entrust the security of her body: the relics of powerful intercessors were, unfortunately, all too sought after by thieves and over-zealous faithful alike. Thus, Clare's remains were interred within the Church of San Giorgio—the same place Francis's body had rested for four years before the completion of his grand basilica on the opposite side of Assisi. Some of the sisters relocated to San Giorgio to be with Clare's body while most of the community remained in San Damiano.

Two months after Clare's death, Pope Innocent IV entrusted the bishop of Spoleto with the process of authenticating Clare's holiness and promoting the cause of her canonization. With the collaboration of two of the closest companions of Francis and Clare, Brothers Leo and Angelo, in addition to an archdeacon, an archpriest, and a notary, the process involved interviews with sixteen of Clare's sisters at San Damiano in addition to four citizens of Assisi who had known Clare or lived with her in her childhood.[212]

Scripture says, "a man will be known through his children" (Sir 11:28). In this case, a woman was known through her sisters. All agreed that Clare had lived a life of heroic virtue and extraordinary holiness. Her youngest sister, Beatrice, summarized Clare's sanctity in a few sentences during her testimony, "In her virginity, humility, patience, and kindness; in the necessary correction and sweet admonition of her sisters; in the continuous application to her prayer and contemplation, abstinence and fasting; in the roughness of her bed and clothing; in the disregard of herself, the fervor of her love of God, her desire for martyrdom, and, most especially, in her love of the Privilege of Poverty."[213]

After their sworn testimony, Archbishop Bartholomew reached the conclusion that everyone already knew: Clare was now glorified with the other saints and angels in heaven. She was indeed a saint.

Pope Innocent IV never saw the conclusion of the canonization process as he died on December 12, 1254. Her canonization, consequently, would be declared by his successor. And the next pope elected was none other than the former protector of the Poor Ladies, Cardinal Rainaldo! Taking the name, Alexander IV, it would be, providentially, Clare's personal friend who would preside over her canonization Mass on August 15, 1255. Since August 11 was already the feast day of the first bishop and patron of Assisi, San Rufino, Clare's feast day was assigned August 12; it was later reassigned to August 11.[214]

Now the woman who spent her life trying to go down and become minor in the world—like her Beloved Spouse—had been, on the contrary, true to her birthright all along: she was always a noble Lady, a Major. Yet her nobility was of a different sort. Now, indeed, she was noble, a Major of the highest order: she was with the saints, the angels, God himself. The cross—death—did not have the final word. The Resurrection did!

Two years after the canonization, Pope Alexander arranged for the property of San Giorgio to be given up by the canon priests to construct a large basilica. Then, in 1259, the sisters who were still at San Damiano united with those already in San Giorgio to form one monastery under one abbess. Their permanent monastery was built, and the San Giorgio chapel was reconstructed into the sisters' prayer choir. The basilica was completed in 1265, and Clare's remains were interred underneath the main altar. In 1850, Clare's tomb was excavated. Her remains were exhumed and a new crypt was constructed, allowing pilgrims to view her body.[215]

Clare—the woman who in life had been veiled and hidden—is now open to the world. Countless miracles occurred at Clare's tomb in the years after her death and many were documented by the author of the ancient *Legend*.[216] And still to this day pilgrims and visitors alike testify to receiving graces, even miracles, at her tomb in Assisi. Her "light from the cloister" is still shining, burning, for all of Assisi and, indeed, the entire world to see.

> O how great is the vibrancy of this light
> And how intense is the brilliance of its illumination!
> While this light remained certainly in a hidden enclosure,
> It emitted sparkling rays outside.
> Placed in the confined area of the monastery,
> Yet she was spread throughout the wide world.
> Hidden within,
> She extended herself abroad.
> Yes, Clare hid, yet her life has come to light.
> Clare was silent, yet her fame was proclaimed.
> She was hidden in a cell, but was known in cities.
>
> FROM PAPAL DECREE OF CANONIZATION, 4[217]

This is the Conclusion of the Legend of the Virgin, Saint Clare.

LEGEND 41:62

What you hold, may you hold,
What you do, may you do and not stop.
But with swift pace, light step, unswerving feet,
so that even your steps stir up no dust,
may you go forward
securely, joyfully, and swiftly,
on the path of prudent happiness,
Believing nothing,
Agreeing with nothing,
that will dissuade you from this commitment [of poverty]
or would place a stumbling block for you on the way,
so that nothing prevents you from offering
your vows to the most high in the perfection
to which the Spirit of the Lord has called you.

EXHORTATION TO AGNES OF PRAGUE: SECOND LETTER, 11–14

AFTERWORD

Father Murray Bodo, OFM

ST. Clare studies have grown beyond my imagining since 1979 when I wrote my first tentative words about St. Clare. Each book on her that came out delighted me, from textual studies, to biography, to this lovely new narrative Bret Thoman has given us. It is a story that incorporates discoveries from the deep well of Clarian research. This is a book that is accessible to anyone who loves a good story, an old-fashioned, well-made story of a love driven by profound contemplation of the Poor Christ of the Gospel.

But the book does more than tell a story. It is an excellent compendium of sources for the life and spirituality of St. Clare and her sisters at San Damiano. It is a readable book that is filled with new and useful information about St. Clare, her milieu, and more particularly, the life and mores of medieval Assisi, the medieval Church, and medieval society. And all of this is contained within a story that begins, as would an historical novel, with these enticing words:

> Early in the morning at dawn, Ortulana was awoken when the first rays of light penetrated the narrow window of her towering castle in upper Assisi. The noblewoman arose and looked out the window to the east, the Orient. The light was just beginning to break through the darkness of the night as the

> sun arose behind the mountain called Subasio. Her city, then known as Ascesi (Ascending), was home to a son who had risen just ten years earlier. His name was Francis. A daughter was about to rise. And her name would be "light." In time, the great son and daughter of Assisi would dispel the darkness of their city and illuminate lands far, far beyond.

That lovely opening paragraph not only gives the reader a sense of presence, of "being there," but the whole of the book foretold. The rest of the book will be an opening up of how that story unfolded, and the narrative keeps pace with whatever new information is given the reader. For example, in keeping with Clare's family being one of knights, when they return to their castle in Assisi after their exile in Perugia, a neighboring city, Thoman relays this significant information:

> As their first objective was defense, they rebuilt their fortified castle next to the cathedral. As knights, the men were well-versed in the art of warfare and military strategy, and they knew how to use their weapons. They had to be ready for war, as another attack against them or Assisi could come without warning, so they trained frequently for battle in tournaments and jousts. They also sometimes joined the ranks of other allied cities when called upon to defend their territories, too.

Besides such concrete material as this, the whole narrative is interwoven with quotes from the first medieval life of Clare, called *The Legend* (meaning "to be read," because it was intended to be read aloud for the edification of the people, who for the most part had no books of their own or could not read).

The biblical "Song of Solomon" is also quoted throughout, and Clare's own writings and the testimony of her own sisters and others are skillfully incorporated into the story to give the book heft and credibility. In addition there is a plethora of endnotes that sort through controversies among scholars about certain facts, or that fill the reader in on matters best inserted into endnotes so as not to interrupt the flow of the narrative.

As the opening paragraph of the book implies, the story of Francis is very much a part of the story of Clare, and Thoman makes Francis's entrance into the story a natural development of where Clare's God-story is leading her. For example, when Clare heard Francis preach,

> Clare was spellbound. She stood there in the cathedral, enraptured as the words of Francis struck her to the core. She had never before heard anyone speak like him before. She had never heard such a sermon about the Incarnation and poverty in that way.
>
> That night, Clare could not sleep as she lay in her bed. She could not stop thinking about Francis. There was something new and inspiring about him. His and the brothers' lives and actions corresponded perfectly to her thoughts about religion and faith. The way he was filled with the spirit was like a magnet, and she felt drawn to him. Francis lived the Christian way of life that had been calling to her.

And from that beginning, the whole incredible story of Clare becoming the first Franciscan woman unfolds in all of its beauty, its difficulties, its conflict with five different popes, and its ultimate confirmation of her and her sisters' way of living in Gospel poverty by Pope Innocent IV two days before she died.

Though St. Clare and her sisters were contemplatives who lived within the enclosure of the monastery of San Damiano, the story of their lives, their struggles and triumphs, is dramatic.

It is an inner journey, a Christian romance as extraordinary as the romance of the Quest of the Holy Grail, and at the same time as extraordinarily ordinary as the lives of Francis and his brothers who, like Christ's knights-errant on the road, carried out daring deeds as they preached and lived out, simply and daily, the Gospel of Jesus Christ.

Father Murray Bodo, OFM

TIMELINE

1194	Clare is born (or 1193)
1199	Civil war erupts in Assisi; Clare's family exiled in Perugia
1204/05	Clare returns to Assisi
1211	Francis and Clare begin meeting secretly
1212	Palm Sunday: Clare leaves her home; receives tonsure in Portiuncula; spends sixteen days in San Paolo of the Abbesses; spends "short period" in Sant'Angelo in Panzo
1215	Fourth Lateran Council in Rome: declares no new religious rules
1215–18	Clare officially designated "abbess" of San Damiano
1218	Clare is subject to the first rule written by Cardinal Hugolino
1219	Clare's sister Agnes leaves San Damiano to start new monastery near Florence
1224	Clare's long illness begins
1226	October 3: Francis dies
1228	Pope Gregory IX visits San Damiano
1228	Clare's youngest sister, Beatrice, and mother, Ortulana, join San Damiano
1235–38	Clare corresponds with St. Agnes of Prague in first three letters
1240	September: Saracens' raid repelled at San Damiano by Clare's prayers

1241	Clare intercedes, thwarting another attack on Assisi by Vitalis d'Aversa
1247	Pope Innocent IV writes a second rule for the sisters
1253	July: Clare's sister Agnes returns from Florence to be with her in her final days
	August 9: Pope Innocent IV approves the Rule of Clare
	August 11: Clare dies
	August 12: Clare's body is moved to San Giorgio. Agnes dies a short time afterward
1255	August 15: Clare is canonized a saint
1260	October 3: Clare's body is transferred into recently constructed basilica
1850	Clare's body is rediscovered beneath the altar
1872	Clare's body is placed in newly constructed crypt

NOTES

PREFACE

1 See Thomas of Celano, *First Life*, ch. 28.
2 She was, indeed, canonized by Pope Benedict XVI in 2010.

PROLOGUE: HER NAME SHALL BE "LIGHT"

3 Mount Subasio stands at 1,290 meters (4,250 feet) above sea level on the western edge of the Apennine mountain range. Assisi is on its northwestern slope.
4 The Roman name for Assisi was "Asisium"; Dante, in Canto XI of *Paradiso* in *The Divine Comedy,* famously referred to it as "Ascesi."
5 The actual family home no longer exists. However, documents in the archives of Assisi attest that its original location was next to the Cathedral of San Rufino. Most likely, the home was farther toward the corner of the cathedral square, which was most likely bigger then.
6 Pietro (a neighbor of Clare) testified, "Lady Clare was noble, of a noble family, and of an upright manner of life. There were seven knights of her household, all of whom were noble and powerful" (Nineteenth Witness, Process, 1).
7 See Twentieth Witness, Process, 3.
8 Though it is impossible to know when she went, we know that Ortulana traveled on pilgrimage to Rome, Monte Sant'Angelo in Apulia, and "beyond the sea," presumably to the Holy Land (see First Witness, Process, 4; *Legend of St. Clare* 1, 1).
9 Several decades ago, the Via Antiqua was renamed Via Francesca, memorializing it as the ancient road that went north toward France.

10 Pacifica was a neighbor and distant relative of Ortulana and Clare. She was the second woman to follow Clare to San Damiano and the first witness in the process of canonization. She testified that she "accompanied [Ortulana] beyond the sea for reasons of prayer and devotion. They also went together to Sant'Angelo and Rome" (First Witness, Process, 4).

11 There is no record that Clare ever left the city of Assisi; however, she did feel that Christians should embrace the spirit of pilgrimage in their lives. She quoted Francis in her Rule using his same words, "Let the sisters not appropriate anything to themselves, neither a house nor a place nor anything at all; instead, as 'pilgrims and strangers' in this world who serve the Lord in poverty and humility, let them confidently send for alms" (Rule of Life, ch. 7).

12 Clare had two younger sisters—Catherine, who changed her name to Agnes, and Beatrice—however, it is unclear if she had brothers or other sisters. Of interest is the testimony of two blood sisters and nuns in San Damiano, Amata and Balvina (the fourth and seventh witnesses in the Process) who testified that they were "blood nieces" of Clare (*nepoti carnali*) and daughters of Lord Martino of Coccorano. Based on their testimony, either Clare had additional siblings or the two sisters were second cousins or relatives. Arnaldo Fortini did not discover any other siblings of Clare; his daughter, Gemma Fortini, researched Clare's life more thoroughly and did not believe she had additional siblings either. Both Fortinis believed that the two sisters, Amata and Balvina, were distant cousins of Clare.

13 This locution is documented by the third witness in the Process, 28, as well as *Legend of St. Clare*, 1, 1. The English translation does not render well the Latin play on Clare's name, which also indicates "light" (*Clara*), throughout the text.

14 The same font can be visited in the cathedral of Assisi. St. Francis was also baptized in it in addition to the first followers of Francis and Clare who were from Assisi. It is unclear if Clare was born in 1194 or 1193.

15 The roots of Clare's name in Latin, *Clara*, mean "clear" or "light."

1 War and Exile

16 It is known that Clare had two younger sisters, but their ages are not known.

17 Although the Majors in Assisi in that era lived in the cities, they owned numerous castles and farms in the countryside.

18 It is not known if Francis participated in the civil war of 1198, as it is not documented in any historical sources; however, many believe he was active in the uprising, as his family would have gained much from it.

19 Sister Benvenuta was the second witness to testify in the process of canonization; she says she had stayed with Clare in the same house before she entered religion (Second Witness, Process, 3); she was the third woman after Clare to enter San Damiano.

20 *Legend of the Three Companions* is the only early Franciscan source to mention this battle but does not name the location.

21 Both Thomas of Celano (second biography) and the *Legend of the Three Companions* wrote that while in prison, Francis was optimistic and joyful by nature, and his fellow prisoners thought he was crazy and admonished him for it.

22 It is documented historically in *Legend of the Three Companions* that Francis fought in the battle of Collestrada against Perugia on behalf of the Assisian army in 1202.

2 Back to Assisi

23 See Seventeenth Witness, Process, 4.

24 Lady Bona, another witness, said, "She [the witness] firmly believed, because of the great holiness of her life that she had before and after she entered religion, that she had been sanctified in her mother's womb" (see Seventeenth Witness, Process, 1).

25 For more on Clare's mother, see First Witness, Process, 4; *Legend of St. Clare*, ch. 2.

26 See Eighteenth Witness, Process, 3.

27 See *Versified Legend of the Virgin Clare*, ch. 5 and *Legend of St. Clare*, ch. 2 for more on her childhood.

28 See First Witness, Process, 3.

29 It is unclear if Clare personally visited the poor or sent alms through intermediaries. The seventeenth witness, Bona, said, "she used to send [food] to the poor … and she testified that many times she had brought it to them"; it is unclear who brought it. The twentieth witness, Ioanni, said that Clare "saved the food she was given to eat, put it aside, and then sent it to the poor." The *Legend*, too, refers to Clare sending food through "intermediaries" (see *Legend of St. Clare* 2:3).

30 See First Witness, Process, 3.

31 See Twentieth Witness, Process, 3.

32 See Eighteenth Witness, Process, 2.

33 Pietro of Damiano testified that Clare's parents and relatives wanted her to "marry magnificently, according to her nobility, to someone great and powerful" (Nineteenth Witness, Process, 2).

34 See Eighteenth Witness, Process, 3.

35 August 11, the feast of the patron of Assisi, was the same day St. Clare would die.

36 Clare had a great devotion to the crucifix; see *Legend of St. Clare*, ch. 20.

37 See Clare's First Letter to Agnes of Prague, 15-17.

3 Francis

38 The voice he heard through the crucifix was an important moment in Francis's life. It is referred to in all the Franciscan sources.

39 This prophecy was mentioned in Celano, *Second Life*, ch. 8, 13, *The Legend of the Three Companions*, ch. 7, and Clare's Testament, v. 12–14.

40 The life trajectory of Valdès (known also as Peter Waldo) began like that of Francis. He was born in 1140 in Lyons, France, and grew up as a wealthy merchant. But after a conversion when he was twenty years old, he gave away his wealth to the poor. After he gained followers, he went to Rome in AD 1179 seeking permission from Pope Alexander III to live his way of life.

He was granted permission to live poorly, but he could preach only if the local bishop permitted it. When the bishop of Lyons denied his request to preach, however, he did so anyway, leading to his group's eventual excommunication.

41 None of Francis's sermons are recorded anywhere. However, we can imagine the content and style of his preaching: Francis said that while preaching, words should be "well-chosen and chaste . . . in a discourse that is brief, because it was in few words that the Lord preached while on earth" Cf. Later Rule, ch. 9, 3.

42 Francis referenced these Scriptures in his First Admonition, 14.

4 The Encounter

43 Witnesses in the canonization process said that Clare entered religion due to the preaching of Francis. Sister Amata, Clare's blood niece and a nun in San Damiano, said, "Through the exhortation and preaching of Saint Francis, [Clare] had assumed religion, even though before she entered it she was considered holy by all who knew her" (see Fourth Witness, Process, 2). Clare also indicated that it was Francis whose example converted her (see Rule of Clare, ch. 6, 1; see also Testament of Clare, 24–25).

44 Clare's sister, Beatrice (who also followed Clare in San Damiano), indicated that it was Francis who sought Clare: "After Saint Francis heard of the fame of her holiness, he went many times to preach to her, so that the virgin Clare acquiesced to his preaching, renounced the world and all earthly things, and went to serve God as soon as she was able" (see Twelfth Witness, Process, 2).

45 Clare called herself the *plantula sancti patris Francisci* ("little plant of Holy Father Francis") in several of her own writings. (See Testament, 37, 49; Blessing, 6; Rule of Life, 1, 3.)

46 The content of the dialogue between Francis and Clare is not recorded anywhere. The *Legend* records simply that Francis "encouraged her to despise the world (*Legend of St. Clare* 3, 5). Bona testified, "[Francis] always preached to her about

converting to Jesus Christ. Brother Philip did the same. She listened willingly to him and consented to all the good things said to her" (Seventeenth Witness, Process, 3).

5 *FUGA MUNDI*—FLIGHT FROM THE WORLD

47 Some believe that Clare left her home in the year AD 1211.

48 It is not known when Clare gave away her possessions. Beatrice testified, "After that, she sold her entire inheritance and part of that of the witness [Beatrice] and gave it to the poor" (see Twelfth Witness, Process, 3); her testimony places the timing after hearing Francis preach and before receiving the tonsure. See also Nineteenth Witness, Process, 2; since Pietro knew Clare in her childhood, this, too, would indicate that Clare's renunciation came before leaving her home. However, the testimonies of nuns Benvenuta, Filippa, and Angeluccia all seem to indicate that Clare was already a nun in San Damiano when she gave away her possessions. Further, the *Legend* introduces it after she is in San Damiano, saying that she sold her paternal inheritance "at the very beginning of her conversion" (see ch. 9, 13). Given the diverse testimonies, it is clear that Clare did, indeed, sell her inheritance; however, it is unclear when. In any case, on the night of Palm Sunday, Clare renounced her status and privileges in addition to her future inheritance.

49 See *Legend of St. Clare* 4, 7 for more on Clare's departure.

50 Some assume that this important historic event took place at San Rufino, as it was the cathedral in Clare's era and next to her family home. However, most scholars believe it took place at the co-cathedral and former cathedral of Assisi, Santa Maria Maggiore, as the bishop's residence was next to it in that time, as it is still today.

51 Bishop Guido personally placing the branch in Clare's hand is documented in *Legend of St. Clare* 4, 7. The gesture suggests that he knew about what was about to transpire, was in accordance with her decision, and possibly had even been involved in the details of her departure.

52 Sister Cristiana, who was living with Clare's family at the time of her departure, testified to Clare's strength: "Because she did not want to leave through the usual exit, fearing her way would be blocked, she went out by the house's other exit that had been barricaded with heavy wooden beams and an iron bar so it could not be opened even by a large number of men. She alone, with the help of Jesus Christ, removed them and opened the door. On the following morning, when many people saw that door opened, they were somewhat astonished at how a young girl could have done it" (Thirteenth Witness, Process, 1).

53 The *Legend of St. Clare* mentions that Clare had a companion, but does not say who (see ch. 4, 7). None of the witnesses in the canonization process, however, mention any companion. The most logical assumption is that it was one of the two sisters, Pacifica or Bona, as they were close to Clare during this period. It could not have been Bona, however, because she testified in the canonization process that she was in Rome at that time "to observe Lent" (see Seventeenth Witness, Process, 5). Therefore, it was probably Pacifica. In fact, Pacifica testified that "she had entered the Order at same time with [Clare], and served her for the most part almost day and night" (First Witness, Process, 3). Nonetheless, it is odd that she would have omitted in the same testimony that she accompanied Clare to St. Mary of Angels.

54 Each of the early Franciscan sources describe the event: on the feast of St. Mathias on February 24, 1208, Francis heard a Gospel reading: "Take no gold, nor silver, nor copper in your belts, no bag for your journey, nor two tunics, nor sandals, nor a staff" (Mt 10:9–10). This is when he donned the crude sandals, penitent's tunic, and the cord, which would make up his habit.

55 The first was San Damiano. The last was a little church known as San Pietro (or Pietrignano) in Spina, not far from Rivotorto; today it is on private property and has once again fallen into ruin.

56 Numerous witnesses indicated that it was Francis himself who gave Clare the tonsure (see XII, 4; XVI, 6; XVII, 5; XVIII, 3; XX, 6). *Legend of St. Clare* indicates simply that her hair was "shorn by the hands of the brothers" (see ch. 4, 8).

57 In Clare's era, the veil had less religious importance for a woman in religious life than today. In the Middle Ages, women of diverse states, including religious, married or unmarried, wore a head covering similar to a veil while in public, and sometimes in private. For the medieval writers of Clare's story, therefore, the emphasis was not on the veil but rather the tonsure that marked her as a consecrated woman. Most likely, her head was entirely shaved.

6 San Paolo of the Abbesses

58 Abbess and prioress are the names for the head and second-in-command in women's Benedictine monasteries; the men's equivalent would be abbott and prior.

59 Choir nuns (*choristae*) went by "donna" in medieval monasteries (in English the title would be "lady"); for men, the title would be "dom." The words derive from *domina* and *dominum* in Latin, meaning "lady" and "lord."

60 "Sister" was the title for lay sisters (*conversae*) in medieval monasteries.

61 The origin of the Rosary began in this period in the monasteries as a prayer alternative for illiterate monks and nuns who could not read the Latin Psalter.

62 Some believe that Clare entered San Paolo as a servant, a *conversa*, because she had had no dowry, which was a requirement for the privilege of living as a *chorista*. Following this hypothesis, it would not have been possible for Clare to have stayed with the *choristae* (see Marco Bartoli, *Beyond the Legend*, ch. 4).

63 It is not sure who was abbess when Clare arrived in 1212. However, a papal bull, dated May 5, 1201 from Pope Innocent III to the nuns of San Paolo is written to the abbess, whose name was Sibilia, and reconfirms various papal privileges.

64 This is taken from the First Admonition of Francis.

65 Clare used these same words in her first letter to Agnes of Prague (see 19).

7 Knights and Nuns

66 None of the sources indicate that Clare's father was present in these encounters; the *Legend*, for example, refers simply to "her relatives." Some historians believe, therefore, that since her father was not mentioned specifically, he was already deceased or was off at battle.

67 Lord Ranieri testified that he had "many times asked her to be willing to consent to [marriage]" (see Eighteenth Witness, Process, 2).

68 Ioanni (John) of Ventura was the only witness to testify to Clare's genealogy, saying, "Her father was called Favarone and her grandfather Offreduccio di Bernardino" (see Twentieth Witness, Process, 2).

8 Sant'Angelo in Panzo

69 The names of the friars are mentioned by Beatrice, Clare's youngest sister (see Twelfth Witness, Process, 5).

70 Sister Angeluccia testified that when Clare sent the extern serving sisters out into the world, she would tell them to "praise God when they saw beautiful trees, flowers, and bushes; and likewise, always to praise Him for and in all things when they saw all peoples and creatures" (see Fourteenth Witness, Process, 9).

71 Beatrice described Clare's departure simply: "Then St. Francis, Brother Philip, and Brother Bernard took her to the church of Sant'Angelo in Panzo, where she stayed for a little time" (see Twelfth Witness, Process, 5). *Legend of St. Clare* says it even more simply: "After a few days [in San Paolo], she went to the church of San Angelo in Panzo" (ch. 4, 8).

72 Today, the property is owned by the heirs of the noble Assisian family Bonacquisti, who purchased the property in 1604. It was wonderfully restored in 1950, and today the grounds are available for receptions, or sometimes, visits.

73 The sources provide no evidence as to why Clare went to Panzo or what type of community was there when she arrived. Modern historians believed that the original convent was built in the

tenth century on the ruins of a Roman villa. The earliest documents attesting to any religious community are from 1232–33 when Panzo was listed among other ecclesial institutions receiving public funds. Some historians believe that, like San Paolo, Panzo was Benedictine (e.g., Sister Battista Alfani, writing in the fifteenth century, claimed it was Benedictine; see also Maria Sticco). Others have suggested it was a type of Beguinage in which the women were *incarcerate* or penitents (see Regis Armstrong, "Clare of Assisi," p. 184, footnote a; Sister Chiara Lainati, "Santa Chiara d'Assisi," pp. 101–109).

74 More specifically, the *Legend* says, "Sixteen days after the conversion of Clare, Agnes, inspired by the divine spirit, ran to her sister [in Panzo]…" (p. 303). This is the only timeframe we have of Clare's movements after she left her father's house, as specific numbers are not given by any of the other witnesses.

75 None of the witnesses of Clare's canonization process mention this event; it is recorded only in *Legend of St. Clare* (ch. 16). Given the specifics therein, it is possible that the author of the *Legend* had interviewed Agnes directly.

76 The *Legend* attests to Francis giving Agnes the tonsure (see *Legend of St. Clare*, ch. 16, 26).

77 Clare's birth sister, St. Agnes, is not the same as St. Agnes of Prague, the Bohemian princess who renounced royalty for a life of austerity following Clare's way of life and with whom Clare corresponded in at least four letters.

78 *Legend of St. Clare*, ch. 4:10.

79 Twelfth Witness, Process, 5. Clare herself later testified in her Testament that before San Damiano, she "lived for a short time in another place" (Testament, 32).

9 San Damiano: Enclosed and Open

80 San Damiano is a lovely sanctuary and is one of the most frequently visited sanctuaries in Assisi. Today it serves as the novitiate for the central Italian provinces of the OFM Franciscan Order and is a place of prayer.

81 It is not known exactly what the church of San Damiano looked like when Clare arrived. Some scholars believe that when she arrived in 1212, the church was long and tall and was comprised of only one floor. They believe that the dormitory (now above the church) and the infirmary (now above the refectory) were added during Clare's lifetime after her community expanded. It is known with certainty, in any case, that the wooden door and rose-window now in the façade, and the portico below, were added well after Clare's death.

82 There is an ongoing debate within Franciscan circles as to whether or not Clare intended to live within the enclosure in the beginning. Some believe that Clare initially intended to live "like the friars" (itinerantly and out in the world) but was forced to accept it with the Rule of Hugolino in AD 1218. However, there is only one ancient source to recount her ever leaving the enclosure (see *Little Flowers of St. Francis*, ch. 15). Yet neither the *Legend* nor any of the canonization witnesses refer to Clare ever leaving San Damiano; on the contrary, they all point to the practice of an enclosure from the outset. In one instance, Sister Pacifica testified that they used to call on Brother Bentevenga to beg alms for them in "about the second year" after coming to San Damiano; i.e., in 1212 or 1213—well before Hugolino's Rule (see First Witness, Process, 15). Further, the regulations of Clare's own Rule regarding the enclosure were stricter than either the Rule of Hugolino or Innocent IV (see ch. 5 and 11). Thus, it is my belief that Clare always intended to live within the enclosure. For a thoroughly scholarly analysis of this viewpoint, see Chiara Augusta Lainati, "The Enclosure of St. Clare," *The Cord*, 28 (1978): 4–15, 47–60.

83 Some have suggested that the religious community in Panzo was a Beguinage (see note 73). It should be noted, as well, that a later group of religious women (active in the 1240s) sought to live even more actively than the Beguines. Drawing inspiration from Francis and the friars (and even Clare herself), they preached in the streets and lived without a fixed residence. Known as "*minoretae*," they were never recognized as a religious order and, on the contrary, were condemned by the pope in the strongest of terms.

84 See Marco Bartoli, *Clare of Assisi*, chapter 4, for more on the enclosure. Bartoli sees the enclosure as having been practiced from the beginning, though he refers to the early experience of Clare as "eremitical." He believes the enclosure eventually became more "monastic" due to subsequent ecclesial directives and rules.

85 Testament, 19–20.

86 Third Letter to Agnes, par. 7. She may have written about the enclosure in other writings, but this is the only incidence that has been conserved.

87 See Rule of Clare, ch. 2. This is a marked difference from the Rule of Hugolino, which permitted a sister to leave the enclosure "only to found another monastery." It suggests that Clare, while fully embracing the enclosure, allowed for some fluidity.

88 This was the first sentence of Clare's Rule.

10 Just One Privilege

89 The heart of Clare's form of life, poverty, is spelled out in her Rule in ch. 6.

90 Fr. Giulio Mancini, OFM, believes that the building that eventually served as the refectory for Clare was once a hospice for pilgrims. In *Il Santuario di San Damiano, Luogo di Spirito*, he refers to it as a place of hospitality for *Romeos*—pilgrims journeying to Rome (see p. 43).

91 Clare wrote in her Rule, "Let the sisters not appropriate anything to themselves, neither a house nor a place nor anything at all; instead, as 'pilgrims and strangers' in this world who serve the Lord in poverty and humility, let them confidently send for alms" (Rule, ch. 7).

92 *Anonymous of Perugia* names the priest (see ch. 1, 7).

93 Fr. Mancini, OFM believes that these rooms became the residence of three or four friars who served the sisters: there was usually a priest, a deacon, and two brothers. Today, the first two of the three rooms are chapels (open to the public) while the third remains a sacristy (closed to the public).

94 Today, the ancient choir exists behind the altar to the right. Originally, however, the choir extended in both directions behind the altar; at some point in history, it was halved due to a later wall being built, probably during the Renaissance.
95 Clare gives instructions on praying in her Rule, ch. 3.
96 Today there is another floor above the church that served as the dormitory; it was likely added during Clare's lifetime. Above the refectory, a floor was added for what became the infirmary. The dormitory can be visited by the public, while the infirmary is part of the enclosure of the friars who reside there. There is also a small chapel along the infirmary corridor named after Saint Agnes, Clare's sister.
97 In chapter 6 of her Rule, Clare wrote, "[the sisters] are not to receive or hold onto any possessions or property. . . except as much land as necessity requires for the integrity and the proper seclusion of the monastery; and this land is not to be cultivated except as a garden for the needs of the sisters."
98 In chapter 6 of her Rule, Clare wrote that the sisters are to be bound to poverty "by not receiving or having possession or ownership either of themselves or through an intermediary." In chapter 8, she adds, "Let the sisters not appropriate anything to themselves, neither a house nor a place nor anything at all."
99 Initially, Clare rejected the title abbess but was later forced to accept it.
100 In Clare's Rule, she wrote, "If she [the candidate] is suitable, let the words of the Gospel be addressed to her that she should go and sell all that she has and take care to distribute the proceeds to the poor" (ch. 2).
101 The friars were often called upon to beg alms for the sisters. Some believe that the friars either already had a small community in San Damiano when Clare arrived or else arrived soon after.
102 Clare dedicated the entirety of chapter 7 in her Rule to the sisters' manner of working.
103 This prayer is mentioned in several ancient manuscripts. They all indicate that Francis prayed it at the foot of the crucifix of San Damiano.

104 Clare used the imagery of the mirror often in her writings. In Testament, 6, Clare described the mission Francis left for her. She wrote that the sisters are to be "mirrors" or examples to themselves and then to others: "For the Lord himself has placed us not only as a form for others in being not only an example and mirror, but even for our sisters whom the Lord has called to our way of life as well, that they in turn might be a mirror and example to those living in the world." This dream is conjecture.

11 Community

105 Sister Benedetta would succeed Clare as abbess after her death; her remains are interred in the Basilica of St. Clare in a side chapel off the nave.

106 In reality, not all women entered right away; at least the following women entered between AD 1212–1215: Bona, Pacifica, Benvenuta, Balvina, Cecilia, and Filippa. It is not known when the others entered.

107 Ortulana joining San Damiano is mentioned by several witnesses (see First Witness, Process, 5; see also IV 37–40 and the Papal Decree of Canonization, 10). It is not known when she entered; Beatrice, who was probably much younger than Clare and Agnes, entered in AD 1229 (and died in AD 1260). It is assumed that Clare's mother, Ortulana, entered at the same time, most likely after her husband, Favarone, died. In truth, the sisters were not reunited in San Damiano, as Agnes was in Florence at this time.

108 From the records of a notary from Perugia, AD 1238, no. 14.

109 See First Witness, Process, 12.

110 See Second Witness, Process, 1–2.

111 See Third Witness, Process, 9.

112 See Fourth Witness, Process, 2–3.

113 See Fifth Witness, Process, 2.

114 See Sixth Witness, Process, 2.

115 See Seventh Witness, Process, 3–4.

116 Clare wrote in her Testament, "When the blessed Francis saw, however, that, although we were physically weak and frail,

we did not shirk deprivation, poverty, hard work, trial, or the shame or contempt of the world—rather, we considered them as great delights, as he had frequently examined us according to the example of the saints and his brothers, he greatly rejoiced in the Lord" (27–28).

117 Later, in 1228, Cardinal Hugolino give them the name, "Order of San Damiano" or "Order of the Damianites." Jacques de Vitry, a bishop and future cardinal, in a letter of 1216 referred to the "Lesser Brothers and Lesser Sisters" while in Perugia and the Spoleto Valley for the funeral of Pope Innocent III. Today the order is known as the "Order of Poor Clares" in English, while in Italian, they are called "*Clarisse*."

118 These are the words Francis spoke to Clare as recorded by her in her Rule (ch. 6, 3–4); see also Thomas of Celano, *Second Life*, 204.

119 This is adapted from Clare's obedience given to Francis in her Rule, ch. 6, 10–14.

120 The names of the friars are listed on a plaque within the courtyard of San Damiano today.

12 The Struggle for San Damiano

121 Brother Philip of Atri (Filippo Longo) was close to Clare and the sisters. While Clare was still in her family home, he accompanied Francis to their secret meetings; later, with Bernard and Francis, he accompanied Clare from San Paolo to Panzo; later still, while Francis was in the Middle East, Cardinal Hugolino appointed him visitor of the sisters.

122 Cardinal Hugolino was a personal friend of Francis and was also the protector of the Franciscan Order. As such, he had a pivotal role in the development of Clare's way of life. On March 19, 1227, he was elected pope, taking the name Gregory IX.

123 Opinions diverge as to the exact year when Clare's sister went to Florence; it was around this time, in any case. Clare remained close to her via letters (none survive) while she was away. She eventually returned to Assisi in the year Clare died.

124 Cardinal Hugolino was a guest at San Damiano in 1220 and wrote Clare a beautiful letter afterward.

125 Saint Benedict was born in AD 480 in Nursia in the region of Umbria. He is considered the father of western monasticism and is the patron of Europe. He made a tremendous contribution to Christianity when he organized monasticism with a Rule. The Benedictine Rule became the principal way religious life was lived in cloistered monasteries for centuries in the West. The monastic orders would dominate religious life until the High Middle Ages.

126 In truth, the distinction between *conversae* and *choristae* remained in San Damiano, though much more subtly, due to the necessity of knowing Latin for prayer. Also, Clare permitted a small number of "extern" sisters (not vowed to the enclosure) to leave the cloister for practical needs. The illiterate sisters and the extern sisters were sometimes referred to as *conversae*. In any case, the enclosed sisters who prayed the Office had no special privileges.

127 In chapter 4 of her Rule, Clare describes how the abbess should govern the monastery. Her description of servant leadership is in line with Franciscan ideals and quite different from the way powerful Benedictine abbots and abbesses commonly ruled over their monasteries in that period.

128 Clare discusses the role of the extern sisters, or serving sisters, in her Rule (ch. 2 and 9). She also dedicates an entire chapter (11) to the role of the "portress" and the importance of guarding the door to San Damiano and keeping the custody of the enclosure.

129 Clare wrote in her Rule, "[A cloistered sister] may not go outside the [monastery] except for a useful, reasonable, evident, and justifiable purpose" (ch. 2). While the monastic tradition prohibited cloistered sisters from leaving the cloister walls unless seeking to establish another monastery, Clare allowed for more flexibility. (Note that here she is not referring to the extern, or serving sister, which she introduced in the same paragraph of her Rule, but to a tonsured, vowed sister.)

130 The Fourth Lateran Council was one of the most important councils of the High Middle Ages. Canon 13 of the council

forbade the establishment of new religious orders. Its prohibition against new orders was part of the struggle against heretical and heterodox movements of the day.

131 The *Legend* mentions how Clare received oral approval for the privilege of poverty from Pope Innocent III (see ch. 9, 14). Other sources refer to it, too.

132 Clare wrote in her Rule, "Blessed Father [Francis] . . . wrote a form of life for us" (ch. 6). She later reiterated in her Testament, "He wrote a form of life for us" (33).

133 Pope Innocent III granted Clare oral approval of her way of life after the Council in AD 1216 with the words, "We confirm with our apostolic authority, as you requested, your proposal of most high poverty, granting you by the authority of this letter that no one can compel you to receive possessions."

134 The teachings of Joachim of Flora and Amalric of Bena were expressly condemned during the Council.

135 These were some of the heterodox, schismatic, or heretical groups in Clare's era that did not remain faithful to the Catholic Church.

136 Clare, like Francis, placed her movement under the obedience of the Catholic Church. In chapter 1 of her Rule, she said, "Clare . . . promises obedience and reverence to the Lord Pope Innocent and his successors canonically elected and to the Roman Church." She also said in her Testament, "I commend all my sisters . . . to the supreme Pontiff, and, especially, to the Lord Cardinal who has been appointed for the religion of the Lesser Brothers and for us" (44).

137 The first witness of Clare's canonization process testified that Clare was forced by Francis to accept the direction and government of the sisters (see also *Legend of St. Clare*, ch. 8, 12).

138 The "Form and Manner of Life" was written by Cardinal Hugolino for the sisters on August 27, 1218.

13 The *Transitus* of Francis

139 See Testament, 48.

140 See Testament, 38.

141 Numerous witnesses referred to this peculiar dream: Sister Filippa described it in detail (see Third Witness, Process, 29; see also IV: 16; VI: 13; VII 10). More than likely it occurred sometime after Francis died.

142 *The Little Flowers of St. Francis* said, "[Francis] visited Saint Clare many times, giving her holy instructions" (ch. 15). *The Little Flowers* was an Italian rendition of an earlier Latin work known in English as "The Deeds of Blessed Francis and His Companions." The earlier work said, "When [Francis] stayed in Assisi, he frequently visited her with his words of sacred encouragement."

143 The following comes from chapter 16 of the *Little Flowers of St. Francis*.

144 See *Little Flowers of St. Francis*, ch. 15. Today, near the Portiuncula, there are bronze statues of Francis and Clare seated together at picnic. This is the only incidence of Clare leaving the enclosure after arriving in San Damiano in any of the medieval sources.

145 Thomas of Celano wrote, "[Francis] gradually withdrew his bodily presence from [the sisters of San Damiano]" (Celano, *Second Life*, ch. 155, 204). In 205–206, he wrote that Francis also asked the brothers not to disturb them.

146 The following account comes from Thomas of Celano, *Second Life*, ch. 157.

147 Thomas of Celano described the stigmata of Francis by saying that the marks in his hands and feet consisted of flesh forming on the palms of his hands and tops of his feet, appearing as black heads of nails; he said that on the opposite sides, flesh formed like the twisted ends of nails (see Thomas of Celano, *First Life*, Book Two, ch. 3). Today, the slippers that Clare sewed for Francis are visible in the reliquary chapel in her basilica.

148 See *Assisi Compilation*, 83.

149 The "Canticle of the Sun" was one of the first poems written in the common language of that time. It is first mentioned in the *First Life* of Thomas of Celano, written in 1228. Fr. Giulio Mancini, OFM, believes Francis wrote it from within the second room to the right of the church, presently the Chapel of the Crucifix.

150 *Assisi Compilation* (ch. 13) and *Mirror of Perfection* (ch. 108) both indicated that the reason Clare could not see Francis was because both of them were ill. Thomas of Celano, however, suggested a different reason, which my account follows.

151 See *Assisi Compilation*, 14.

152 Francis died on the night between October 3 and 4. However, in those days, the next calendar day began at sunset, not midnight.

153 The following account of the end of Francis's life is taken from Thomas of Celano, *Second Life*, ch. 162, as well as Bonaventure, *Major Life*, ch. 14.

154 This story about "Brother" Jacoba and the almond treat (*mostacciolo* in Italian) is recounted in "Legend of Perugia," 101.

155 Brother Elias of Cortona was one of the first friars to join Francis. He became the minister general in AD 1221, succeeding Peter of Catani.

156 *Assisi Compilation*, 13, said that Francis wrote Clare a letter, which he gave to a friar saying, "Go and take this letter to Lady Clare, and tell her to put aside all her grief and sorrow over not being able to see me now. Let her be assured that before her death, both she and her sisters will see me and will receive the greatest consolation from me."

157 There are three ancient written accounts documenting Francis's body being carried to San Damiano: Thomas of Celano *First Life*, Part 2, ch. 10; *Mirror of Perfection*, 108; *Assisi Compilation*, 13. The scene is also portrayed pictorially in one of the Giotto frescoes in the upper basilica of St. Francis. There are noteworthy differences in the three accounts: Thomas of Celano says that Francis's body was laid in the church and the sisters looked at him from within the enclosure through a window that was opened for the occasion; *Assisi Compilation* and *Mirror of Perfection* both say that his body was brought directly to the grille and the bars were removed so the sisters could be close to him; the Giotto fresco, however, depicts his body in front of the church of San Damiano, with the sisters not only outside the enclosure but outside the church as well.

158 Thomas of Celano wrote about how Francis believed that spiritual union with the sisters was more important than "bodily

presence." He says this is why he kept his presence from them (see Thomas of Celano, *Second Life*, ch. 155; par. 205–207).

14 "Gaze, Consider, Contemplate, and Imitate"

159 Numerous witnesses testify to Clare appearing radiant and full of light after prayer (see Fourth Witness, Process, 4; see also II 59; VI 10; IX 38; X 37–40; XVIII 7).

160 See *Legend of St. Clare*, ch. 13 for more on Clare and prayer.

161 *Legend of St. Clare* has an entire chapter dedicated to Clare's love of the cross (20). She also wrote often about the cross in her letters to Agnes of Prague (see I 13–14, 18; II 19–21; IV 23–27).

162 Clare wrote these four words in her Second Letter to Agnes of Prague, "O most noble Queen, gaze [on Him], consider, contemplate, desiring to imitate your Spouse." In her Fourth Letter, she expounded on the four words in the entirety of her letter. Since almost twenty years had passed between the two letters, it is believed that Clare reflected on the words for that time. These four words have been suggested as a Poor Clare method of prayer similar to the four-step monastic method of *lectio divina*. The four letters written to Blessed Agnes are extremely rich in spirituality, and they are the best sources that reveal Clare as a mystic and contemplative.

163 See Fourth Letter, 22.

164 See First Letter, 19–21.

165 See Third Letter, 21–26.

166 See Third Letter, 13–14.

167 For more on the theological concept of divinization, see Catechism of the Catholic Church: 460, 1988.

168 See Testament, 5:19–20.

15 Saracens

169 See *Legend of St. Clare*, ch. 12 for more on Clare's mortifications. Francis also intervened during her illness, forcing Clare

to use a straw mattress instead of one made of twigs (see Tenth Witness, Process, 7).

170 See Mt 26:6–13; Mk 14:3–9; Jn 12:1–8.

171 From the time of Charlemagne in AD 800 until the unification of Italy in AD 1861, the popes had a dual role: spiritual headship of the Catholic Church in addition to temporal ruler over the Papal States throughout central Italy.

172 Saracens were generally understood to be Arabs or Muslims. Some, however, believe that the term *Saracen* did not necessarily refer to an Islamic soldier but was a derogatory term referring to anyone—Christian or Muslim—who fought as an unprincipled mercenary.

173 The Saracen attack against San Damiano was testified to frequently by the witnesses in the canonization process (see III: 18; IV: 14; VI: 10; VII: 6; IX: 2; X: 9; XII: 8; XIII: 9; XIV: 3). It also takes up an entire chapter in the *Legend of St. Clare* (14).

174 Sister Francesca offers the most detailed description of the attack (see Ninth Witness, Process, 2); the following account draws from her description as well as the *Legend.*

175 Sister Francesca testified that she and another sister named Illuminata heard the voice but that Clare had ordered them not to say anything about it while she lived.

176 Sister Cecilia, Sister Balvina, and Sister Beatrice all testified that Clare had a desire to be a martyr in Morocco—the Holy Land (see Sixth, Seventh, and Twelfth Witnesses in the Process).

177 See Fourth Witness, Process, 14.

178 The *Legend* says the event took place simply by "the door" and tradition has placed Clare appearing from the dormitory. However, the wooden door off the dormitory was placed there by the friars well after Clare's death to memorialize the event. Sister Francesca, however, specified that the event took place by the door in front of the refectory. An ancient stairwell descends from the infirmary down to the door by the refectory just off the courtyard; this is the most likely site where Clare was positioned when the Saracens entered the cloister.

179 See Testament of Francis, 10.

180 See *Legend of St. Clare*, ch. 18, which deals exclusively with Clare's devotion to the Eucharist.

181 The door the Saracens broke through (or went over) was probably in the same place as the door to the left of the church that enters into the courtyard today.

182 Due to this event, Clare is often depicted in iconography holding up the Eucharist in a monstrance. However, the monstrance was not used until the fourteenth century when popular devotion to the Blessed Sacrament increased. In Clare's era, it would have been conserved in a pyx.

183 A second incursion against Assisi took place in summer, 1241. Clare's response to it was described by numerous witnesses as well as the *Legend of St. Clare*, ch. 15. Vitalis d'Aversa, a captain under the imperial army, was sent by Emperor Frederick to sack Assisi. After being asked to pray for Assisi's safety, Clare scattered ashes on her head and the heads of the sisters and prayed for Assisi. The next day, the army left without incident.

16 THE *TRANSITUS* OF CLARE

184 Sister Pacifica said that Clare had been sick for twenty-nine years (see First Witness, Process, 17), while the *Legend* says she had been sick for twenty-eight years (see *Legend of St. Clare*, ch. 26, 39).

185 See *Legend of St. Clare*, ch. 24, 39.

186 See *Legend of St. Clare*, ch. 24, 37. This episode has been referred to as a hunger strike. Together with her fierce defense of poverty, it shows that there were some things Clare refused to mitigate; both demonstrate the tenacity of her character and how she was not afraid to confront those with authority over her.

187 Apart from the four letters we have which she wrote to the former princess of Prague, Blessed Agnes, Clare also wrote letters to Ermentrude of Bruges, in addition to Francis and Cardinal Hugolino; these latter are not conserved.

188 See *Legend of St. Clare*, ch. 7, 11.

189 See Second Witness, Process, 18.

190 See Third Witness, Process, 15.
191 See Fourth Witness, Process, 11.
192 See Ninth Witness, Process, 6.
193 See *Legend of St. Clare*, ch. 22, 32.
194 Numerous witnesses testified to these healings (see First, Second, Third, and Fourth Witnesses; see also *Legend of St. Clare*, ch. 22).
195 See First Witness, Process, 15.
196 See Sixth Witness, Process, 16.
197 This was the Christmas Mass of 1252 (see *Legend of St. Clare*, ch. 19; see also Third Witness, Process, 30). It was also mentioned, though in less detail, by the fourth and seventh witnesses.
198 *Little Flowers of St. Francis* said, "St Clare . . . was so holy, that not only the Bishops and Cardinals but the Pope himself wished to see and hear her, and went often to visit her in person" (ch. 33).
199 See *Legend of St. Clare*, ch. 17, 27.
200 See *Legend of St. Clare*, chapter 27; Third Witness, Process, 24.
201 See *Little Flowers of St. Francis*, ch.33. The name of the pope is not mentioned.
202 For more on Clare's obedience to the pope, see Rule of St. Clare, ch. 1; Testament, 44.
203 Chapters 6–8 in her Rule pertain to poverty.
204 The following account of her death is taken from *Legend of St. Clare*, 29.
205 Agnes died "a few days later" (*Legend of St. Clare*, 48) or on November 16 (according to tradition).
206 Sister Filippa described how the event unfolded (see Third Witness, Process, 32).
207 Sinibaldus Fieshi was Pope Innocent IV.
208 The Rule that Clare wrote had already been accepted in the name of the pope roughly one year earlier by Cardinal Rainaldo, the protector of the Poor Ladies. However, it was Clare's desire for the pope himself—as a sign of the Church's unity—to personally accept her Rule, which he did.
209 The original manuscript was lost until AD 1893 when the abbess of the Basilica of St. Clare, Sister Rossi, discovered it in a sealed box with other items of Clare.

210 This vision is recounted by Sister Benvenuta (from Assisi, not Perugia) who testified to seeing it herself (see Eleventh Witness, Process, 3–5); the *Legend* refers to the same vision, but the seer is anonymous (see *Legend of St. Clare*, ch. 29, 46).

Epilogue: Light Shines Again —From San Domiano to San Giorgio

211 The following account comes from *Legend of St. Clare*, ch. 30.

212 The Process of Canonization was lost to history and was only rediscovered in 1920. The accounts given in the Process, together with the *Legend* (which narrates stories so similar to the accounts of the witnesses that its author had surely interviewed them), provide vital firsthand information about Clare and are both indispensable sources for knowledge of her life.

213 See Twelfth Witness, Process, 6.

214 For centuries Clare's feast was celebrated on August 12; however, in the years following Vatican II, her feast was moved to August 11.

215 Clare's remains are enclosed within a ceramic replica inside a glass coffin. Originally, Clare's face was covered with a leather mask. However, in the most recent restoration, an entirely new ceramic mask was digitally constructed to correspond with her bone structure; this is the face of Clare seen today (her skeletal remains can be seen only from within the monastery). On the other side of the crypt is a museum housing a number of relics and artifacts from the lives of Francis and Clare. The original San Damiano crucifix hangs in a chapel to the right of the basilica (what used to be the Church of San Giorgio).

216 See *Legend of St. Clare*, ch. 31–40.

217 The author of the decree poetically and skillfully used Clare's Latin name, Clara (also meaning "light"), in nineteen different ways.

FOR FURTHER READING

Armstrong, Regis J., ed. and trans. *The Lady: Clare of Assisi: Early Documents.* Hyde Park, NY: New City Press, 2006.

Bartoli, Marco. *Beyond the Legend.* Translated by Frances Teresa Downing. Cincinnati: St. Anthony Messenger Press, 2010.

———. *Clare of Assisi.* Quincy: Franciscan Press, 1993.

Bodo, Murray, and Susan Saint Sing. *A Retreat with Francis and Clare of Assisi: Following Our Pilgrim Hearts.* Cincinnati: St. Anthony Messenger Press, 1996.

Carney, Margaret. *The First Franciscan Woman.* Quincy, IL: Franciscan Press, 1993.

Delio, Ilia. *Clare of Assisi: A Heart Full of Love.* Cincinnati: St. Anthony Messenger Press, 2007.

Downing, Frances Teresa. *This Living Mirror.* Maryknoll, NY: Orbis, 1995.

Fortini, Arnaldo. *Francis of Assisi.* Translated by Helen Moak. New York: Crossroad, 1980.

Fortini, Gemma. "The Noble Family of St. Clare of Assisi," *Franciscan Studies* 42 (1982): 48–67.

Lainati, Chiara Augusta. "The Enclosure of St. Clare," *The Cord* 28 (1978): 4–15, 47–60.

Miller, Ramona. *In the Footsteps of Saint Clare: A Pilgrim's Guidebook.* St. Bonaventure, NY: The Franciscan Institute, 1993.

Peterson, Ingrid. *Clare of Assisi: A Biographical Study.* Quincy, IL: Franciscan Press, 1993.

ACKNOWLEDGMENTS

IN writing this book, I am first and foremost indebted to those who were my Franciscan formation ministers: Cricket Aull, OFS, and the late Father Linus Desantis, OFM Conv. (1943–2015). From them I learned about Francis and Clare not just by listening to their teachings but more so by observing them as they "preached the Gospel at all times and when necessary used words."

This book would not have been possible without the laborious research of Father Regis Armstrong, OFM, who, in his unparalleled book *Clare of Assisi, The Lady, Early Documents*, translated into English and edited all of Clare's extant writings in addition to other medieval sources relating to her. I also drew from Marco Bartoli's groundbreaking work *Clare of Assisi* (1993) in addition to his follow-up *Beyond the Legend* (2010).

Next, a special thank you goes out to the reviewers of this book who invested much time critiquing it and improving it with keen observations and insightful feedback: Sister Ilia Delio, OSF, Sister Ramona Miller, OSF, Joanita Nellenbach, OFS, Sister Ann Bremmer, OSF, Sister Kathy Warren, OSF, Sister Bernadette Cappola, OSC, Father Murray Bodo, OFM, and Professor Marco Bartoli.

Gratitude is in order for the community of San Damiano, particularly the guardian, Father Giampaolo

Massotto, OFM, for granting me "behind-the-scenes" access, and Brother Eunan McMullan, OFM, for showing me around (Irish brogue and all!). It was a singular joy to listen to the nonagenarian and former provincial minister of Umbria, Father Giulio Mancini, OFM, as he graciously placed his ninety-five years of erudition, wisdom, knowledge, and kindliness at the service of this book.

Thanks also go out to the Benedictine monks of Norcia (Nursia) and Father Basil Nixen, OSB, who evaluated my less-than-flattering treatment of Benedictine life in medieval Italy. And he made the time to do this from within makeshift wooden housing after the monks' ancient church and monastery, built over the birthplace of St. Benedict, collapsed during the earthquakes of 2016.

In the spirit of Franciscan *minoritas*, last but not least, I wish to thank the Poor Clare sisters of San Severino and Camerino for making time to write the Foreword. I am grateful to them for all the inspiration I have received through them, for their support in my endeavors, and for their friendship. My prayers are with them, as (like the Benedictines) their monasteries, too, were damaged by last year's quakes, and they—like so many religious communities in central Italy right now—have been forced to respond to those same words that moved St. Francis over eight centuries ago: "Go and rebuild my church, which, as you can see, has totally fallen into ruin."

Finally, I would like to thank my family, who listened as I read this book out loud: Katia, for supporting and loving me in this endeavor; Iacopo, for listening patiently; and Claremarie, to whom this book is dedicated, for appreciating it and even offering her own feedback and critiques!

Spread the Faith with . . .

TAN • BOOKS

A Division of Saint Benedict Press, LLC

TAN books are powerful tools for evangelization. They lift the mind to God and change lives. Millions of readers have found in TAN books and booklets an effective way to teach and defend the Faith, soften hearts, and grow in prayer and holiness of life.

Throughout history the faithful have distributed Catholic literature and sacramentals to save souls. St. Francis de Sales passed out his own pamphlets to win back those who had abandoned the Faith. Countless others have distributed the Miraculous Medal to prompt conversions and inspire deeper devotion to God. Our customers use TAN books in that same spirit.

If you have been helped by this or another TAN title, share it with others. Become a TAN Missionary and share our life changing books and booklets with your family, friends and community. We'll help by providing special discounts for books and booklets purchased in quantity for purposes of evangelization. Write or call us for additional details.

TAN Books
Attn: TAN Missionaries Department
PO Box 410487
Charlotte, NC 28241

Toll-free (800) 437-5876
missionaries@TANBooks.com

TAN·CLASSICS

A collection of the finest literature in the Catholic tradition.

978-0-89555-227-3

978-0-89555-154-2

978-0-89555-155-9

Our TAN Classics collection is a well-balanced sampling of the finest literature in the Catholic tradition.

978-0-89555-230-3

978-0-89555-228-0

978-0-89555-151-1

TAN·BOOKS

978-0-89555-153-5

978-0-89555-149-8

978-0-89555-199-3

The collection includes distinguished spiritual works of the saints, philosophical treatises and famous biographies.

978-0-89555-226-6

978-0-89555-152-8

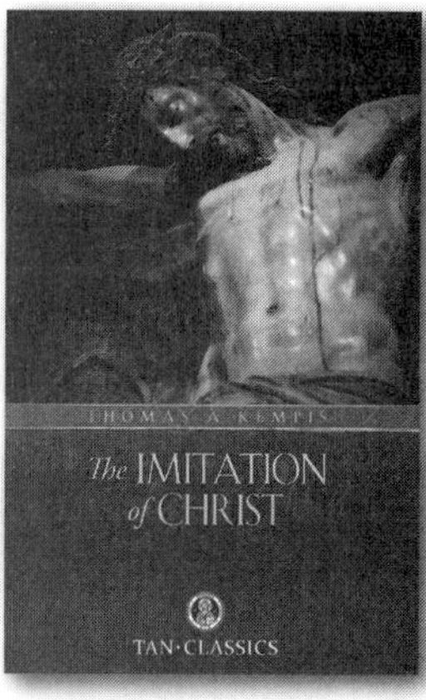

978-0-89555-225-9

Visit us at TANBooks.com

JOY : 01736 369369

TAN · BOOKS

TAN Books is the Publisher You Can Trust With Your Faith.

TAN Books was founded in 1967 to preserve the spiritual, intellectual, and liturgical traditions of the Catholic Church. At a critical moment in history TAN kept alive the great classics of the Faith and drew many to the Church. In 2008 TAN was acquired by Saint Benedict Press. Today TAN continues to teach and defend the Faith to a new generation of readers.

TAN publishes more than 600 booklets, Bibles, and books. Popular subject areas include theology and doctrine, prayer and the supernatural, history, biography, and the lives of the saints. TAN's line of educational and homeschooling resources is featured at TANHomeschool.com.

TAN publishes under several imprints, including TAN, Neumann Press, ACS Books, and the Confraternity of the Precious Blood. Sister imprints include Saint Benedict Press, Catholic Courses, and Catholic Scripture Study.

For more information about TAN,
or to request a free catalog, visit
TANBooks.com

Or call us toll-free at
(800) 437-5876